MW00435796

The Walkthrough

Insider Tales from a Life in Strategy Guides

By Doug Walsh

Also by Doug Walsh

Fiction

Tailwinds Past Florence

✄

Non-Fiction

One Lousy Pirate

This is a work of creative nonfiction. Events, descriptions, and conversations are portrayed to the best of the author's memory. All characters, incidents and dialogue are real. Some names and identifying details have been omitted or obscured to protect the privacy of the people involved.

Cover and book design by Scarlett Rugers of TheBookDesignHouse.com

Printed and bound in the United States of America

Published by Snoke Valley Books
P.O. Box 654
Snoqualmie, WA, USA 98065

Visit www.dougwalsh.com

For everyone who made BradyGames the best

damn strategy guide publisher there was.

Introduction

Chicago, 2003

I sat at an airport bar nursing a hangover after a weekend spent attending ballgames with a motley mob of lifelong friends, each of them single and eager to party. Our annual ritual. Hours earlier, we had bro-hugged our goodbyes and split up to return to our separate corners of the country. I was alone in taking a flight westbound, to Seattle, home to my wife and dogs. My only memory of the prior forty-eight hours was Ozzy Osbourne leading Wrigley in "Take Me Out to the Ballgame."

As I prodded tomato-tinted ice cubes with a celery stalk, a guy in a tailored suit took the empty stool beside me. Hair slicked back, a little gray around the temples, he ordered whiskey. Neat. Or maybe I'm making that part up. I don't remember. Does it matter?

He unbuttoned his suit jacket and launched into the standard litany of airport banalities. Was I coming or going? What brought me to

Chicago? How long was I in town? Then, failing to sense my boredom, he asked what I did for a living.

"I'm a writer."

"Oh, really? What do you write?"

This is where it gets tricky. Though I'd been authoring video game strategy guides for only three years at that point, I'd had enough of these conversations to know my honest response would trigger one of two reactions. The person asking would find it absolutely fascinating, admit to being a gamer, and then barrage me with questions. Or, every bit as likely, they'd emit a dismissive snicker and tell me their kid should come help me one day. I glanced downward and, guessing the guy's shoes cost as much as a first-class upgrade, figured he'd choose option two—and that I'd have to counter by asking how many times his kid had written a two-hundred page book in three weeks.

What followed was an hour of the most thoughtful, intelligent conversation I've ever had about strategy guides with someone who didn't work in this niche industry. He thought it fascinating that games had gotten complex enough to warrant their own how-to books, but seemed to understand why modern software companies wouldn't have the time or resources to create the books themselves. The man asked a number of questions about process, dealing with beta code, licensing rights, and the logistics of multiplayer. Just as I began to think he might have been looking to bankroll his own publishing imprint, he stood to leave. But not before suggesting I write a book about my experiences one day.

And that's what I did, setting to work the morning after the announced closure of Prima Games in November 2018.

The Walkthrough: Insider Tales from a Life in Strategy Guides is a memoir and a love letter. It's a collection of anecdotes and an insider reveal. It's a look back at my life as a gamer, my career writing strategy guides, and the highs, lows, and rewards that came with the job.

For eighteen years, I was one of the most prolific authors of video game strategy guides for BradyGames and Prima Games, with over one hundred guides to my credit. This book is my story.

Falling into It

Cyclists like to say they all belong to one of two clubs: those who have crashed and those who will. I don't know how many can say their accident directly led to them discovering their dream job, but I suspect I'm in rare company.

My world froze between takeoff and impact one Thursday evening in the spring of 2000. The details of that interstitial moment seared themselves into my memory, scarring me, guaranteed to forever bubble from my persona like a cattle brand. First there were the vibrations, as faint as a mouse crawling within a wall, as the shoe disengaged from the pedal. Then my head and torso fell forward, limp, as if I'd reached for a step that wasn't there. A flash of amazement followed as I sensed my foot performing the impossible, slipping between my aerodynamic cycling wheel's spokes.

Then came the cartwheels.

My left shoulder slammed first, snapping my collar bone in three as the bike, still attached to my left foot, sailed into the Carolina sky. I flew with it, across the country road's center-line, bouncing, tumbling, and grimacing in agony, convinced I'd shattered my ankle. My cycling kit split wide, leaving me exposed to God and hog farmer alike. My entire left side, from shoulder to knee, resembled prime rib cooked rare and seasoned with chip-seal.

It wasn't until later, after asking if my bike was okay; after a friend whistled dramatically and reported my 33-mph crash speed; and after my wife, some two dozen cyclists behind me, choked back tears as she described seeing it happen in slow motion, that I realized how lucky I was no cars were coming the other way. Someone in the group had a cell phone—a rarity back then—and an athletic trainer who worked the sidelines for East Carolina University's football team ran interference, minimizing the manhandling I received from the corn-bred paramedics who hoisted me into the ambulance. A few hours spent alone, shivering, picking road grit from my skin on a gurney in a hospital hallway, proved to be the worst of it. My ankle was merely bruised, the road rash would heal, and the arm sling would come off eight weeks later.

I was less than a year into my first real job, serving as a technical writer/illustrator for a forklift manufacturer. The pay was lousy, but I couldn't afford to be choosy after abandoning graduate school with a perfect GPA through four semesters and no respect for the program. My Master's thesis concerning Beaufort County's groundwater geochemistry would forever lay unfinished. So it goes, as Vonnegut might say.

A week into my convalescence, I peeled my t-shirt free of the weeping road rash and fetched the mail. A get-well card from my father had come. Tucked inside it were a gift card to GameStop and a handwritten note instructing me to get a new game, on him, since the crash waylaid my upcoming triathlon season. I hadn't touched my PlayStation in months, still furious after a third-party "mega" memory card devoured seventy hours of save data for *Final Fantasy VII* and *Metal Gear Solid*. I never did beat either of those games, but I stood alone in mourning the loss. My wife had threatened to leave me if she ever heard the Chocobo racing music again. Crisis averted.

So, I drove across town to GameStop, a store I seldom frequented given there was an Electronics Boutique much closer—a detail I mention only to underscore how serendipitous the coming moment was.

After browsing for far too long, with nothing really grabbing my attention, I settled on *NHL Faceoff 2000*, a hockey game. While I stood waiting for the clerk to retrieve a copy from the locked display case, I noticed a stack of postcard-sized advertisements on the counter.

Are you good at video games?

Yeah, I thought, I'm pretty good.

Can you write well?

I just earned an "A" in a Scientific Manuscripts class if that's what you're asking.

Are you comfortable working independently under tight deadlines?

I shrugged a response. I was twenty-four years old and could only gauge my abilities by my studies and athletic achievements, nothing professional yet. But I'd long romanticized the notion of the harried writer, up all night under deadline, guzzling coffee and Scotch, fingers dancing across the keys. The thought of being able to add video games to that image felt downright pornographic, like George Costanza sneaking a pastrami sandwich beneath the sheets. I stood there, eye-banging the advertisement as drool dribbled onto my arm sling, ignoring the clerk asking for payment, studying every detail of that postcard.

The ad was from a local guy with connections in the industry. He was taking on more strategy guide projects than he could handle and needed to subcontract them out. Those interested were instructed to email him a sample walkthrough chapter for any game of their choosing, six to ten pages. Screenshots optional.

I sped home in my Isuzu Rodeo, mentally browsing my PlayStation collection, trying to settle on the right game, the perfect level. Something not too cumbersome, a sequence conducive to a few paragraphs of general advice followed by targeted tactics for a handful of objectives or mission goals. Bulleted lists and a pop culture reference or two would be ideal. How I knew this, I can't say. It was as if an innate knowledge had lain dormant within me, waiting for this opportunity to kick down the door and announce itself present.

Two years later, before driving that same SUV across the country to move closer to Nintendo's American headquarters, I sold my copy of *NHL Faceoff 2000* at a yard sale, still in its original shrink-wrap.

* * *

I can still picture the rainbow of Atari 2600 boxes stacked tall in my father's hands as he carried them down to our New Jersey basement on Christmas morning of 1982. My brother and I followed in our matching Star Wars pajamas, arguing over which we would play first as my father lit the kerosene heater. The box art for *Demon Attack* and *Atlantis*—two of my favorite games of that generation—looked sinister, too adult for my brother who wouldn't turn three years old for several weeks. The explosive primary colors of *River Raid* won out and the three of us spent the ensuing hours, much to my mother's dismay, passing the joystick back and forth, monitoring our fighter jet's fuel levels while blasting enemy craft out of the air.

Our family was always the last to arrive at my grandparents' house for Christmas breakfast.

I didn't just grow up in a game-playing house; our basement was a veritable arcade. We weren't wealthy—nobody in the blue-collar town of Carteret was—but we never lacked for fun. Though the day-to-day collection varied throughout the years, each of the following found its way into our game room: a 1970s-era pinball machine, full-size air hockey table, nine-foot shuffleboard table, ping-pong table, an imported apanese pachinko machine, a bumper pool table, a dartboard, and a shooting gallery for my dad's collection of air rifles. No, there wasn't much room to walk.

My godmother had me playing backgammon while most kids my age were still hooked on *Hungry, Hungry Hippos*. And though I never did get to join in the family's all-night pinochle sessions before distance, death, and divorce brought them to a close, I'll never forget finally being deemed old enough to play *Risk* with my uncles and grandfather. It's a memory triggered whenever I hear the famous warning from *The Princess Bride* to "never get involved in a land war in Asia."

Still, it was the Atari 2600 (technically the woodgrain Sears Tele-Games Video Arcade) that I enjoyed most. We had dozens of games for the system and, though I was vaguely aware of the ColecoVision and Commodore 64's more sophisticated offerings, the Atari 2600 was all I ever needed. That is, until I experienced the life-altering joy of playing *Super Mario Bros.* and *Duck Hunt* at a family friend's house during the summer of 1987.

Like so many other kids my age, after much begging, bartering, and badgering, my mother relented and got me the Nintendo Entertainment System (NES) as a twelfth birthday gift that fall. Then, thanks to a paper route and a Machiavellian approach to justifying an ever-increasing allowance, I spent the next four years accumulating—and beating—over sixty games for the system. I was a Nintendo fiend, slurping bowls of Mario cereal as I memorized every issue of *Nintendo Power* and *Electronic Gaming Monthly*. I bribed bullies with tips on punching out Mike Tyson and directions through the Death Mountain maze of *Zelda II: The Adventure of Link*. My grades plummeted, and I never did my homework, but it didn't matter. I had found my calling.

Armed with my NES Advantage joystick controller, I quickly became the kid my mother's friends would call when their own children were stuck in a game, usually the seventh dungeon of *The Legend of Zelda* (nobody could ever find the hidden staircase leading to the boss). Together with my newly gained step-brother, Butch, we devised a way to auto-level on the opening screen of *Rygar* by using tape, rubber bands, and the Advantage's turbo button. Then there was the time we spent an entire night on the phone, playing through the notoriously confusing *The Goonies II*, me in the role of navigator, wielding a copy of *The Official Nintendo Player's Guide*, widely considered the first strategy guide ever published outside Japan.

Even in the eighties, quality video game maps were indispensable.

My father installed a Sega Master System at his house and Santa added the battery-draining Sega Game Gear to my arsenal at home, but the NES dominated my tween-age years. The discovery of girls and varsity sports eventually lured me away from video games during high school and college, but not before I paired my love of gaming with a passion for reading. Stephen King and the aforementioned Kurt Vonnegut were my favorites. And it was thanks to their books that I got the notion to one day become a writer. More specifically, I wanted to write for *Nintendo Power*.

But that was in 1989. What teenager didn't want to work for Nintendo back then?

* * *

Doubt crept in as I nosed the car into the parking spot assigned our townhome, the forgotten copy of *NHL Faceoff 2000* beside me on the passenger seat. Was I still any good at games?

There was one.

Aside from a brief fling with my roommate's Super NES during my freshman year of college—nightly hockey tournaments, anyone?—I effectively skipped straight to the PlayStation era.[1] My wife and I married the summer after graduating college, in 1997, and bought a PlayStation that winter, along with a copy of *Cool Boarders 2* and *Bushido Blade*. It was fun, but games were expensive and with non-deferred student loans chewing up half of the meager income I earned as a graduate assistant, new purchases were infrequent, to say the least.

---

[1] Skipping the Super NES generation would be a major hole in my gaming resume throughout my career, but one that was eventually rectified in 2017. That summer, I was hired to capture the screenshots for Prima Games' *Now You're Playing with Super Power* book, written by Sebastian Haley. This required playing through, in their entirety, all of the first-party games that appear on the SNES Classic mini-console, released later that year. I experienced an entire generation's greatest hits in a three-week binge, from *Earthbound* to *Super Mario World* and everything in between.

I made do with the demo discs that came packaged with *Official PlayStation Magazine* and offered at Pizza Hut restaurants. And no demo did I play more than the one featuring the Warehouse level of the original *Tony Hawk's Pro Skater (THPS)*. For hours I sat, playing the same two-minute demo, listening to Goldfinger's "Superman" on infinite repeat as I strove to collect the S-K-A-T-E letters and Secret Tape without bailing, playing the level over and over in an effort to top my previous score. It was enough to make my wife miss the Chocobo theme.

As a former skater long hoping for a proper follow-up to the classic titles *720°* and *T&C Surf Designs*, there was no stopping me from being first in line to buy a copy of *THPS* when the stores opened on August 31, 1999.

And there I was, eight months later, anxious to fire it up once again. Memory, both photographic and muscle, kicked in and it was mere minutes before my Tony Hawk avatar was ready to drop in at The Mall, the level that would serve as the basis for my walkthrough sample. I paused the game, grabbed a pad and pen, and rummaged for the three strategy guides I had in a closet. The guidebooks for *Age of Empires*, *Final Fantasy VII*, and *Myst* were little help to me in providing suitable examples of how one might organize a walkthrough for a simple game like *THPS*.[2] Yet, by paging through those books, and studying the writing

---

[2] The original guidebook for *Myst*, one of the best-selling strategy guides of all time, was written by Rick Barba. I was fortunate enough to finally work with Rick on the *Diablo III* strategy guide in 2012. I suspect Rick Barba stands alongside Tim Bogenn as the only two strategy guide authors with more books to their name than me.

and how the manuscripts were structured, I realized I had little to be nervous about. I knew I could do it.

I hit the record button on the VCR, grabbed the DualShock controller off the floor, and got to work.

I've been writing ever since.

1-900 Daikatana

That weekend, I found myself sitting across from Tim Bogenn at a Bear Rock Cafe, completely overdressed in Dockers and polo shirt, arm still in a sling, ignoring my roast beef and cheddar as I laughed my way through an interview, unable to conceal my giddiness. We hit it off immediately, and the more he described the situation, the more I felt as if I'd stumbled into a dream. I was a twenty-four-year-old grad school dropout who once dreamed of writing for *Nintendo Power*, in the process of winning a job writing strategy guides from home.

Pinch me, I thought.

Tim had recently moved to North Carolina after working in Sony's California offices following the PlayStation launch. In addition to parlaying the Sony gig into an annual contract with market-leading strategy guide publisher, BradyGames, he headed east with a steady stream of writing assignments for IGN, Daily Radar, GameSpot, and GameSpy, as well as the company that handled the scripting of 1-900

p lines. He had too much of a good thing going. The dot-coms kept him
oo busy—and he wasn't one to leave money on the table.

That's where I came in.

To know Tim is to understand that behind the mischievous
smile and beneath the ever-present baseball cap is the mind of a man
who knows how to hustle. I'd go on to work with numerous people during
my career, including at least a dozen other authors, but none could
match Tim's brute-force work ethic. He was hungry, always keeping one
eye on the day's task, the other hunting for tomorrow's opportunity. And
that meant passing along some online gigs to a few lucky newbies and
reaping a cut off the top.

I knew I wouldn't be the only one he was considering, but I was
determined to outwork the others from day one. I just needed that first
chance to prove myself.

Tim liked what he saw from the *Tony Hawk's Pro Skater* sample
and agreed to try me out on a scripting project for those 1-900 lines
gamers used to call when they got stuck. It was for a PC game releasing
that week, a first-person shooter with a funny name I'd never heard of.
The good news was that there'd be an official strategy guide available,
so I'd have help. The bad news was that I seldom played shooters. When
it came to PC gaming, I was more *RollerCoaster Tycoon* than I was
Quake and *Doom.*

That would all change with time. I'd later write the official
guides for a number of shooters including the entire *Bioshock* series as

well as *Halo: Reach*, among many others, but it's a damn good thing m
earliest work was anonymous.

* * *

"John Romero's gonna make me his bitch."

My wife stopped drying the pot in her hands and made a face.
was the look one makes while watching a dog eat its own poop. It was
also the proper adult reaction for anyone outside gaming coming in
contact with the infamous advertisement for *Daikatana*, my very first
gaming assignment.

I'd spent the afternoon scouring websites I never visited before
for news about this game I never heard of. What I learned, aside from
the fact that I'd been living under a rock, was that *Daikatana* had been
delayed repeatedly, its developers were the subject of intense scorn and
derision, and that a recent demo had barely managed twelve frames pe
second. Those still clutching the belief that the game would be a
success placed their optimism in the pedigree of the man in charge,
John Romero, a developer whose resume boasted credits including
Wolfenstein 3D, Doom, and *Quake*.

Whether or not the game was any good didn't matter to me. No
yet. I had other things to worry about. Namely, making sure I had a PC
capable of running it. *Daikatana* was a 3D first-person shooter that ran
on the *Quake II* engine. Unlike the other PC games I owned, there was
no way this one would run on an integrated graphics chip, at least not or

low-end late-nineties Gateway. It was time to wade into the murky, headache-inducing world of turn-of-the-century 3D accelerator cards.

Before I could worry about the hassle of getting a new video card to work, I had to address the cost. Things weren't as tight for us as they were when I was in grad school, but splurging on a new video card was no trivial matter, especially for a job I'd yet to earn a penny from. Luckily, I married a gal raised on the belief that it took money to make money, and she was fully supportive of the purchase. That she'd yet to ever see me fail certainly benefited my cause.

So, I headed to Electronics Boutique and bought an early model 3Dfx Voodoo3 on sale, a copy of *Unreal* to test it out—my first of hundreds of expensed video games—and then, because I had no idea what I was doing, I bought a joystick.

Yes, like one would use for a flight simulator.

My ignorance of the superior controls afforded by mouse and keyboard was absolute. I'd never played *Doom* or *Wolfenstein* or any of the other classic first-person shooters of the 1990s, for that matter.[3] When I heard that *Daikatana* was a "shooter," my mind immediately

---

[3] Ironically, my first real experience with a game in the *Doom* franchise was the terrific 2016 reboot, *DOOM*. I was called upon to write the multiplayer section of the official guidebook. I had just returned home after two years of travel (a mini-retirement) and was rusty as hell. I only had a week to get it done, and only bots to play against, but I managed. I seldom bought the games I wrote guides for, but one exception was *DOOM*. I tore through the campaign and logged an unhealthy number of hours on the multiplayer, which if you ask me, was far better than popular opinion would have you believe.

thought of a joystick. Why? Joysticks have triggers. Triggers are used to shoot. This logic is unassailable.

I was back at the mall a few days later to buy *Daikatana*, the official strategy guide by Prima Games, and to return one lightly used joystick.

With the game slowly installing and the first of hundreds of dinners growing cold downstairs, I set aside the scarlet box with the Japanese kanji emblazoned across it and turned to the strategy guide. Thumbing through it, I quickly came to a fold-out poster, not of the character art or maps, but a pinup of the strategy guide's author. All cleavage and plastic guns, Romero's girlfriend and developer, Stevie "KillCreek" Case, stared from the tri-fold with bedroom eyes, fingertips brushing against her barely concealed beasts.

To see this poster now, in 2019, is a cringe-inducing reminder of how much the world has changed in so little time.

But to the younger me, bouncing on the balls of his feet with excitement, on the verge of a writing career that would ultimately outlast the publisher of that very book, the Stevie Case poster only added to the grandeur of the moment. It told me *Daikatana* was a big deal. And I was about to be a part of it. Sort of.

Writing the script for 1-900 tip lines was not glamorous work, nor was it terribly obvious how to proceed, at least not once you advanced past the initial structure.

Press 1 for help with the Kyoto, Japan levels.

Press 2 for help with the Ancient Greece levels.

Etc.

Beyond that, the inability to share screenshots or point to a map quickly becomes debilitating, especially when offering tips for a high-speed game with minimal visual landmarks, few boss enemies, and scant secrets. Which isn't to say the game was easy. Hell no. *Daikatana* was one of the hardest games I'd ever played at that point (NES classics like *Mega Man* and *Ghosts 'n Goblins* aside), due in no small part to the frustrating jumping puzzles, restrictive save system, and brain-dead "sidekick" characters.

For every tip I wrote about weapon choice or finding hidden Mana Skulls, I wrote another half dozen advising players on getting their AI companions, Mikiko and Superfly, into an elevator without getting stuck. It's the only thing I remember about the game.

Two weeks and twenty-four levels later, I submitted the text document and promptly uninstalled the game, relieved to be done with it. Tim wrote back the following morning to offer me a few hundred dollars more to repurpose it into a full-fledged guide for IGN, screenshots included.[4] Like I said, the man was always on the lookout for opportunities.

---

[4] While writing this chapter, I was astonished to discover that my nearly twenty-year-old walkthrough is still preserved on IGN's website, available as a downloadable PDF. One look is all it takes to realize that it was obviously my first paid writing gig. I clearly struggled to find a balance between too much hand-holding and too little tactical advice. In fairness

* * *

I turned around the *Daikatana* walkthrough in a few days' time, earning myself a month's worth of grocery money and another project from Tim, again for IGN. My next guide was for *Covert Ops: Nuclear Dawn,* a PlayStation game every bit as forgettable as its generic title suggests.[5] A stealth adventure that took place almost entirely on a train, it was essentially a poor-man's *Metal Gear Solid.* It wasn't a glamorous project (neither was *Daikatana*, in hindsight) but *Covert Ops* taught me a valuable lesson. Thanks to it, I learned early in my career to be wary of games with multiple endings. From a consumer's perspective, they're a fantastic proposition and offer plenty of replay value. However, from a strategy guide author's point-of-view, they're an immense time suck and a source of anxiety. No matter how helpful the rest of the guide is, it only takes one missed ending scenario to attract a cascade of angry comments.

The flowchart I created for the *Covert Ops* guide, detailing how to trigger each ending, took dozens of hours to figure out. Quite literally, several days of work went into a single paragraph's worth of text. I sure hope someone read it.

---

though, this is an issue that continued to challenge even the most seasoned strategy guide authors.

[5] Actually, the game was originally called *Chase the Express* in Japan, but Activision changed the name to *Covert Ops: Nuclear Dawn* upon acquiring the North American distribution rights. Sugar & Rockets, the game's developer, was a second-party Sony developer in Japan.

It may sound quaint now, nineteen years later, in the era of hopeful content-creators being paid in exposure in lieu of dollars, but I poured everything I had into each of those early projects, believing every assignment would get me noticed, build my reputation, and effectively be an audition for the projects to come. I was still working four ten-hour shifts a week at the forklift plant, but I was young and sleep was optional. So, I worked late into the night and cranked away nonstop on weekends, determined to transform this freak opportunity into a career.

The extra money was nice, but every time my eyes settled on the *Final Fantasy VII* strategy guide resting atop my bookshelf, I was reminded of the ultimate prize. I wanted a contract with BradyGames.

That goal became a bit more attainable in July 2000, when Tim needed an emergency co-author to meet a deadline.[6] He was weeks into writing the official guide for *Tenchu 2: Birth of the Stealth Assassins* and, unbeknownst to him or any of the editors at BradyGames (communication with game publishers has always been incomplete at best), a third playable character, Tatsumaru, became unlocked at the completion of the main game. Surprise! With the various so-called

---

[6] In a peculiar bit of symmetry, my penultimate project for Prima Games (post-merger with BradyGames) was also of the emergency co-author variety. Work on the *Mega Man 11: Thirty Years of the Blue Bomber* book was comically behind schedule, and the bulk of the hundred-plus pages allotted to the franchise retrospective had yet to be written. The book was going to print in a week's time. My *Mega Man* experience was limited to the original NES game and a brief fling with *Mega Man: Battle Network* on the Game Boy Advance. But, as in any other industry, sometimes the ability to reliably get something done on time is more important than expertise.

"peripheral" chapters still unfinished, not to mention a robust level editor to cover, there was no time for Tim to play, map, and write strategy for an additional seven missions.

Following his instructions, I dusted off my *THPS* sample chapter and emailed it to Leigh Davis, then Editor-In-Chief at BradyGames. She replied with an offer and a Non-Disclosure Agreement for me to sign. A pre-release copy of *Tenchu 2* would arrive the following morning, she said.

This was it. My big chance.

Tim lent me an aging, blue, debugging PlayStation capable of playing unreleased games so long as it was placed upside down on a table. Nervous excitement kept me awake through the night, and every sound had me running to the window, hoping to spot the delivery man as if he were Santa Claus himself. There was zero chance of me going to work in the morning.

The thing about bonus characters is that there's a general assumption that the player has already mastered every aspect of the game before they become available. In the case of *Tenchu 2*, that meant playing through the campaigns of the two main ninjas. I had a copied game save, no prior experience with the franchise, and mere days to get the job done.

Not only were Tatsumaru's missions the most difficult in the game—I blitzed through the other characters' campaigns to "get good" as gamers now say—but this morsel of opportunity coincided with the only time my father and his family ever drove down from New Jersey to

sit during the five years I lived in North Carolina. I spent as much time
s I could with them, including an anxiety-inducing day trip to the Outer
anks that I could ill-afford, but my need to work on the strategy guide
idn't go over well. In hindsight, we should have rescheduled. In reality, I
arricaded myself in my office and left my young wife to play host.

It wasn't the last time I had to prioritize meeting a deadline over
omething fun, but I made a point to never let work interfere with family
bligations again. Sorry, Dad.

The *Tenchu 2* strategy guide was my fourth video game
ssignment since discovering Tim's help-wanted postcard at GameStop.
 would complete sixteen additional projects over the ensuing five
nonths, including IGN guides for *Hitman*, *Shenmue*, and the sprawling
Dreamcast role-playing game *Grandia II*.[7] The *Grandia II* guide took me
ver 150 hours to complete, dropping my thousand-dollar payday into

---

Few franchises captured my heart as much as *Shenmue* had. Though I
never had the chance to write an official guidebook for any of the games
n the franchise, I played through the imported PAL version of *Shenmue*
II for the Sega Dreamcast and, again on the Xbox, falling in love with
Shenhua as she and Ryo walked the lengthy riverside path at the
conclusion of the game. And then, eleven years later, in 2015, I wept
with joy while watching the announcement that *Shenmue 3* would finally
be made. And after running through the house like a crazy person, I
plunked down a hundred dollars on Kickstarter. I tried to convince the
folks at Prima Games in 2018 to commission a "Making of Shenmue 3"
book, but the sales team didn't believe there was enough of a market
for it. Ultimately, it didn't matter, as Prima Games ceased to exist
months before the game released, assuming it doesn't get delayed
again.

the realm of minimum wage, but I didn't care. I was getting paid to play and write about video games.

And I was busy.

Thanks to me knowing the guy who seemed to know everyone else, I was often asked to repurpose material for a different outlet. Tip line scripts would be repackaged as a strategy guide for GameSpy or IGN. The official guidebooks we wrote would be stripped bare, rewritten and paired with new screenshots, then sold to a dot-com in a ghastly breach of contract.[8] It was an incredible way to make a living.

As it turns out, though, not everyone shared this dream—or the ability.

The PlayStation 2 launched that fall and video game fever swept the world. There was dot-com money to burn and it was an arms race for content. Tim's contact at IGN was throwing so many projects our way that I ultimately set out to discover my own sub-contractors to outsource to. I had no idea what kind of cut Tim was taking off the top of the projects I handled, but a small finder's fee felt fair. I reached out to a number of people who had written some of the better GameFAQs at the time, but only two were interested. Most were content doing it as a hobby, didn't think they were good enough, or just didn't have the time. I can appreciate all those concerns, but I still couldn't believe so many people were willing to turn down a paying gig, only so they could do the same task for free.

---

[8] I did this four times, back when I was starting out, and always felt uncomfortable about it. Not enough to turn down the offer, but...

But that's the Internet for you.

Of the two I hired, one slaved away for weeks writing IGN's guide for the real-time strategy game *Sacrifice*, only to decide the money wasn't nearly worth ever doing it again. The other, Michael Lummis, did a bang-up job writing IGN's guides for *Star Trek: Elite Force* and *Black & White* before the whole thing came crashing down in 2001.

The fire hose we were drinking from the prior fall had gone dry. Though a trickle of projects from GameSpy continued to flow the first half of 2001, it wasn't long before the official guidebook publishers were the only paying job in town. Every week brought news of another gaming site turning off its servers. The Internet had killed off the remaining 1-900 businesses. And mega-sites like IGN had undergone massive layoffs and shifted the bulk of their writing internally. It was time to panic.

But that's getting ahead of myself ...

It's-a Me, Mario's Neighbor

Tim stopped by my house one day in August 2000, sporting a sly grin reminiscent of the old Sonic the Hedgehog cartoons. He clearly knew something I didn't, but that was often the case. I remember letting my dogs into the yard as he casually brought up my childhood dream of writing for *Nintendo Power*. I handed him a beer, wondering why he would mention such a thing. Attempting to quote what he said next was every bit as impossible that night as it is nearly two decades on. His words left me in a state of euphoria, feeling like a minor leaguer getting his first call-up to the show. In short, Tim's co-author for *Banjo-Tooie* had to back out and BradyGames had given him permission to offer me the job. The catch: it would require two weeks on-site at Nintendo of America's headquarters in Redmond, Washington.

Saying no was never a consideration, although saying yes meant quitting my day job.

Not only would the project pay more than I'd make in two months designing instruction sheets for assembly workers, but it was also a chance to finally visit Seattle, home of Pearl Jam, Alice in Chains, and Nirvana. The soundtrack of my formative years.

First, I had to get my wife's blessing. That night, over dinner, she listened attentively as I gave her the hard sell. Then she took a deep breath. The corners of her mouth curved nervously upward as she exhaled. Her eyes glistened with a mix of trust, pride, and reluctance. It was a look I'd come to see a lot over the years. She said she hoped I knew what I was doing. That made two of us.

From the moment Tim and I left the tiny Greenville, NC airport, I felt part of an elite squad, specialists flown in to do an impossible task. This is absurd, I know, and more than a small bit nerdy, but I was a wide-eyed twenty-four-year-old, clutching his contractor badge as if it were a Golden Ticket and Nintendo my chocolate factory.

The truth, however, was that Nintendo's old headquarters building was only marginally nicer than the industrial one I had quit the week prior. A sea of clunky white and beige cubicles stretched from end to end, looking no different than the set from the movie *Office Space*, only dimmer. Dated. Aside from the small Nintendo museum, the conference rooms named after characters, and the closet-sized company store that resembled the neon-lit arcades of my New Jersey youth, there was little to suggest that the work performed here could remotely be related to entertainment.[9]

Though disappointed to see how decidedly ordinary the space was, I had plenty of more important things to worry about. For starters, there were the technical aspects of working on-site. Before ever boarding the plane, I'd spent half my compensation on a new laptop, Sony MiniDV camcorder, and enough video tapes to record twenty hours of Jinjo-hunting gameplay (additional trips to Circuit City in search of extra MiniDV tapes were a weekly occurrence). New equipment required a new workflow, which led to learning new software. I used ACDSee to manage the thousands of screenshots I'd capture from the MiniDV tapes, Adobe PhotoShop for designing and placing map callouts, and I wrote the text in Microsoft Word. Ironically, Word was the one with the steepest learning curve thanks to having to decipher the BradyGames style template.

The fire-drill nature of the preceding *Tenchu 2* project had left me no time to learn the specialized template, but that was an exception I'd never be granted again. Unlike the standard template most are accustomed to using, the infamous "Global.dot" contained dozens of

---

[9] Nintendo more than rectified this problem with their current headquarters building, as I was happy to learn when I returned in 2017 to assist with the *Splatoon 2* strategy guide. The building I first visited in 2000 has since been leveled and is now an employees-only soccer field. Their new building welcomes visitors with natural light, gargantuan character statues, eye-pleasing displays showcasing new releases, and a company store I found hard to not to shop in daily. It's a place in which anyone would be happy to spend eight hours a day.

reset styles, each with its own code, formatting, shortcut keys, and purpose. It packed everything from headers to tip boxes to captions and sidebars. It wasn't enough to come up with helpful gameplay tips; authors had to devise the book's layout. The template was how we conveyed our vision to the designers, at least in terms of organizational structure. It was up to them to make it pretty.

Years from now, when I'm on my deathbed and can't remember my birthday or the name of my robot butler, I have no doubt I'll be able to recall the three-key shortcuts to every format in that template.

With Radiohead's newly-released *Kid A* looping infinitely on a pint-sized Sony boombox, we spread out across the Koopa Troopa conference room and got to work. There was Tim Bogenn and me, the authors; Alex Garner, a founder of IDW and the most talented illustrator I ever worked with; and Tim "Fitzy" Fitzpatrick, project editor extraordinaire on hand to, apparently, babysit us.[10]

A problem immediately presented itself: Nintendo made only two N64 development consoles available. Alex needed one to map the game's intricate 3D levels, which meant we authors would have to share one console. Whether this was due to a shortage of hardware or limited supply of game cartridges, I don't know, but I'd encounter this problem in a dozen studios throughout my career. More often than not, game

---

[10] Years later, I learned that some authors needed the babysitter. One in particular had grown so sloth-like in his performance that Fitzy and fellow editor Ken Schmidt had to assume authoring duties when it became apparent that the writer would rather read *Sports Illustrated* than write the book he was hired for.

publishers would insist we work on-site for security reasons, only to the be completely unprepared for our scheduled arrival.

I grasped the oddly-shaped N64 controller—my first time ever handling the so-called batarang—and practiced shifting my hands across its trident-like prongs, reading its buttons like Braille in attempt to decipher how it was intended to be held. More than anything, I wanted to make a great first impression, especially with our editor looking on, but I could sense my confusion showing. Fitzy picked up another controller and positioned his hands on the middle and right-hand grips, completely ignoring the controller's left wing. "Like this," he said, allowing the implied *dumbass* to go unspoken.

I was off to a great start.

Normally, when multiple authors were assigned to a project, one person (often considered the "lead" on the book) would handle the entire walkthrough (the step-by-step guide to the single-player campaign), while the other covered the various systems, enemies, weapons, skills, and items chapters. Because time on-site was limited and the game was filled with hundreds of collectibles, as most 3D platformers of the N64 generation were, Tim and I had no choice but to tag team the walkthrough. We spent the first day learning how to control the bear-bird duo of Banjo and Kazooie, debating which collectibles needed to be mapped, and generally falling in love with the game as we journeyed from Mayahem Temple to Witchyworld and beyond.

Come morning, after a couple of breakfast sandwiches at the Mario Cafe, we started fresh game saves and put our twin camcorders to use leapfrogging one another as we worked our way through the game. One would write strategy for a level while reviewing the gameplay footage on his camcorder's flip-out screen. Meanwhile, the other would spend the day playing the game, recording footage of the next level.[11] Then we'd swap.

It was awkward—especially once we realized there was a fair bit of Metroidvania-style backtracking for previously inaccessible collectibles—but we got the entire 160-page book written in two weeks' time. The process yielded one of the fastest-written books I'd ever worked on, but I can only imagine how disjointed it may have felt for readers, given that Tim and I had quite different writing styles.

We would employ this same approach several months later for *Conker's Bad Fur Day*. But, in an odd sense of symmetry, seventeen years would pass before I again split a walkthrough with another author. Those with a copy of the Prima Games guide to *Super Mario Odyssey*, my final strategy guide for a Nintendo title, may notice a slight shift in voice following the chapter for New Donk City. Though my good friend

---

[11] The issue of taking screenshots and recording gameplay footage was always a sensitive one. Most game publishers and developers knew they could trust us. Even those that insisted on us being on-site for security reasons would turn a blind eye to the fact that we would walk out the door each night with dozens of hours of gameplay footage in our possession. Some developers would forbid us from taking screenshots or recording footage until they got publisher approval, a process that would often take days. In those situations, we simply did what we had to on the sly, draping a jacket over the camcorder or minimizing the video capture screens on our laptops. We could appreciate their concerns, but we had a job to do. And very little time to do it.

Joe Epstein and I each had our own consoles to work from, it would have been impossible for one person to cover all 880 Power Moons in a timely manner. So, I took the first eight kingdoms and Joe handled the rest.

The problem with this approach is that it effectively left me having played only half of three of the best games to ever release on a Nintendo console.[12] Then again, this was a small price to pay for not having to cover the maddeningly difficult Darker Side of the Moon level. Talk about dodging a Bullet Bill!

Another challenge with working on those early first- and second-party Nintendo titles, and every one that followed, was that we were forbidden from using the word *kill*.[13] This rule applied even to a foul-

---

[12] I'm often asked if I continued playing a game after having written the strategy guide for it. The answer is no, but for a couple of reasons. For starters, I was often already working on another strategy guide when the game released—strategy guides were completed more than a month prior to a game's launch. The other reason is that I was often burned out with a title by the time it released. The two major notable exceptions to this were *Halo: Reach* and the *Gears of War* franchise. I worked on the guides for every game in the *Gears* series (yes, including the under-appreciated *Judgment*) and, with *GOW4* being the only exception, I logged hundreds of hours playing multiplayer with friends after each game's release. As someone who almost exclusively handled these games' single-player campaigns, I couldn't wait to finally get a chance to play the multiplayer after the game's release.

[13] Nintendo was far from the only licensor to have strict rules about what can and can't be included in a strategy guide. Another example concerns screenshots of Ferraris and Lamborghinis in racing games. When writing the guide for *Project Gotham Racing 4* (one of my all-time favorite franchises), I was forbidden from including a screenshot

mouthed, satirical game like *Conker's Bad Fur Day*, in which one of the multiplayer modes featured stuffed bears named Tediz sniping unarmed rabbit refugees named Frenchies. Yes, despite the gore, the piss and sex jokes, and a boss named The Great Mighty Poo who serenaded the player with a song about his anus, even then using the word *kill* was *verboten*. Virtually any other synonym was acceptable, from bludgeon to massacre to maim and flay. Nintendo's sensitivity didn't stop there, however. The entire time we were on-site writing the guide for *Conker's Bad Fur Day*, a game made famous for the way it unflinchingly recreated the brutality of the Normandy beach landing scene from *Saving Private Ryan*, we were prohibited from opening the blinds or cracking the door. Nintendo officials didn't want any employee passing by to be offended— even those on the sidewalk outside.

And, as much as it sucked for our editor to be stuck watching us work, thumbing through magazines for two weeks in the pre-smartphone days of yore, I was really glad Fitzy was there. One of the biggest challenges in adjusting to the freelance lifestyle was the lack of personal interaction with my employer. It's one thing to get an email saying I did a nice job; it's another thing entirely to eat three meals a day with your editor, hear his explanations in person, and be able to look him in the eye and know he means it when he says he's going to recommend you for future work. If Fitzy and I weren't friends by the end of the *Banjo-*

---

showing both brands of automobile. The reason? Both manufacturers had a rule requiring that their car always be shown in first place.

Tooie project, we certainly were by the time we wrapped up *Conker's Bad Fur Day* in early 2001.

And not a moment too soon.

* * *

Despite having worked on four official guidebooks and nearly twenty other strategy guide projects, my situation had grown desperate by spring. I had abandoned graduate school in 1999 and quit a reliable job in 2000, only to find myself an indirect casualty of the dot-com collapse less than a year later. IGN had ceased sending projects our way and it was all I could do to not email Leigh Davis at BradyGames every week, asking for work. And by *email*, I really mean *call*.

As anyone involved in the world of publishing can attest, there are few faster ways to get on an editor's bad side than by calling them to beg for work. But that's exactly what I did. And Leigh, every bit the no-nonsense editor-in-chief, eventually challenged my devotion to the profession. How serious was I, she wanted to know, given that I didn't bother attending E3.

For reasons I can't recall, probably a combination of cost and naiveté, I never considered attending the 2001 Electronics Entertainment Expo in Los Angeles. That I should have was news to me. But after tripping over my words, gamely trying to defend my faux pas, I realized that the time for waiting around, hoping work would come my way, was over. I could no longer afford to rely on chance co-authoring

gs or being called on to help in a pinch. Nor could I count on Leigh to
ot screen her calls going forward.

Sensing the conversation speeding to an end with no new
ssignments coming my way, I suggested flying out to meet her and the
ntire BradyGames staff at their Indianapolis offices. We picked a date
he following week and I quickly hung up the phone before she could
hange her mind.

My goal for the meeting was, obviously, to land some work. But I
vas thrilled to meet Leigh and the other editors in person. I fancy myself
 pretty affable guy and I had to believe any chance to make a personal
connection would only help my cause. I knew the editorial staff held
veekly meetings to report the statuses of active projects and discuss
ipcoming titles. I wanted as many people recommending me for those
inassigned books as possible.

So, I flew to Indianapolis and spent the better part of a day
vinding my way through Brady's crowded offices, smiling at the
collections of action figures standing sentry atop monitors, sneaking
glances at the printed galleys sprawled across the tables, and meeting
many of the people I would come to work with throughout the rest of my
career, including a few who hung around until the lights turned off in
2019. In a single day's time I'd gone from feeling like a complete
stranger, begging for scraps, to a part of the team, even if only on the
periphery. I was thrilled.

The trip not only earned me a wealth of new contacts and the *Mario Kart: Super Circuit* project, but I also received a crash course in how the strategy guide business functioned.

People would often ask me why game companies didn't produce the strategy guides themselves. Of all the questions I fielded over the years, this was among the most common, second only to the always pleasant "Do you really get paid to play games all day?" The answer is quite simple. Game publishers—even behemoths like Activision and Ubisoft—were not in the business of selling books. They had no need to staff an imprint's worth of authors, editors, and designers for what may only amount to one or two book projects a year, especially when companies like Prima Games, BradyGames, Versus, and Piggyback were willing to pay them for the pleasure.

In exchange for early access to the game, art assets, and a modicum of support, strategy guide publishers would line up to secure the exclusive licensing rights for a particular title.[14] In the past, game companies often negotiated multi-game agreements that required strategy guides be published for unpopular games in order to land the

---

[14] Back in the rebellious nineties, BradyGames and other strategy guide publishers embraced unofficial guides to eliminate licensing fees and royalties, streamline projects (no time-consuming approval process), and to ensure content wasn't censored. BradyGames branded these guides "Totally Unauthorized" and, befitting the era, created a mascot named Brady, an obnoxious dude in a backwards ballcap and flannel shirt. Readers can glimpse this atrocity by performing an image search for Brady's *Totally Unauthorized Guide to Donkey Kong Country*. You've been warned.

big fish. This was particularly common during the PlayStation 2 era, when each of the major guidebook companies published more than a hundred books a year and game companies took larger risks on unproven properties. For example, in 2001, in order to secure the rights for *Metal Gear Solid 2: Sons of Liberty*, BradyGames agreed to also publish a guide for the dead-on-arrival *Frogger: The Great Quest*.

As the industry matured during the Xbox 360 generation, long-term relationships and multi-game contracts took a back seat to enormous checks. Bidding wars and elaborate pitches involving million-dollar licensing fees and escalating royalties became the norm. This was especially true for blockbuster franchises like *Grand Theft Auto, Final Fantasy,* and *Halo.*[15] And as the bids grew ever higher, the likelihood of turning a profit, especially on a guide for multiplayer-centric first-person shooters, dwindled. With wholesale copies being sold to retailers at 50% off the sticker price, and printing, shipping, overhead, and royalties eating up much of the remainder, the sell-through required to turn a profit became harder and harder to achieve. It wasn't unheard of for a company to sell 150,000 copies of a book and barely break even. One could count the number of annual titles capable of supporting such on

---

[15] Given the rave reviews our *Halo: Reach* strategy guide received, a project for which I wrote the single player content, I was surprised to learn that BradyGames failed to win the rights to *Halo 4*, its sequel. As described to me, our contact at 343 Industries did in fact want us to do the guide, so much so that BradyGames was given a chance to increase their initial bid. They did, upping it to $1.5 million (plus royalties). Sadly, it still wasn't enough, as Prima's initial bid was believed to be $2.0 million, a sum they most likely failed to recover.

one hand. And though there were times when losing a bidding war may have been a blessing in disguise, the failure to secure the rights to *Red Dead Redemption 2* likely hastened the closure of Prima Games.

But, as I sat across from Leigh Davis in 2001, secretly wondering why a strategy guide would be needed for a Game Boy Advance title like *Mario Kart: Super Circuit*, I learned that a number of guides were published at a loss each year in order to guarantee access to the more desirable titles. It's also why we strategy guide authors were paid a flat fee in lieu of the typical advance-and-royalties system.[16] Not only did this prevent authors from refusing to work on titles they knew weren't going to sell, but a book's success had very little to do with the author byline anyway. It was all about the game. They could have hired Stephen King and John Grisham to write the *Conker's Bad Fur Day* guide, but it still wouldn't have outsold a poorly-written *Pokémon* book.

Naturally, the gamer in me wanted to write the guides for the best titles, but I knew I had to start small—handheld *Mario Kart* small. Fortunately, with Nintendo's GameCube console on the way that fall, I was about to position myself to get my pick of the projects just as Nintendo's release schedule heated up.

---

[16] Back in the 1990s, during the strategy guide industry's infancy, a few lucky authors signed traditional publishing contracts, earning royalties on their guides. The publishers quickly reversed course, shifting to a flat-fee system, when one such author began receiving six-figure royalty checks for what amounted to little more than a month's work on a popular guide. The publisher then had an internal employee make some minor revisions to the book and unethically re-released it with a new ISBN to put a stop to the hefty royalty payments.

* * *

Seattle has a reputation for being perpetually cloaked in mist, a drizzly, traffic-snarled city where people live under constant threat of sprouting moss while waiting for the bus. At the risk of earning the scorn of native Seattleites (as rare a breed as Sasquatch, himself), I must confess that the region's rain-soaked infamy is exaggerated. There is at least three months' worth of pleasant weather each year, non-consecutively of course.

It was on one such day in May 2002 that I stood beneath a cloudless sky atop the parking garage at Safeco Field, home of the Seattle Mariners, and called my wife. It was the single most important conversation of our young marriage.

I slowly spun in place as I described the steel blue Olympic Mountains across Puget Sound, snowcapped Mt. Rainier to the south, and the jagged ridge of the Cascade Range to the east. A chill breeze blew from Elliot Bay, and I shivered as I took a nervous breath and spoke the words that would change our lives forever: "I'm not coming home."

I was back in the Pacific Northwest to write the guide for *Eternal Darkness: Sanity's Requiem*, a GameCube title, and, as was so often the case, our Nintendo contact wasn't ready for me to begin. Instead of setting up my equipment and learning the controls, I was told to take in a ballgame and come back tomorrow. So, I attended my first-ever Major

League Baseball game and, in the process, got the idea that this, the Seattle area, is where we should live.

We'd been discussing relocating for nearly a year. To a place with mountains and higher-paying jobs, somewhere we wouldn't be harangued for not attending church or putting off raising a family. Washington State seemed to fit the bill perfectly.

For two weeks, I spent the days documenting my path through the horror-filled corridors of *Eternal Darkness*, trying my best to remain calm as the game's fourth-wall-shattering "sanity effects" tricked me into thinking my controller was broken, the television malfunctioning, or that my save data had been deleted. I counted down the hours each day, anticipating the nightly calls to my wife back in North Carolina, to the ongoing discussion about a move west.

It wasn't only that I thought the area would be a better fit for us I was also certain the move would benefit our careers. After all, BradyGames had a number of Nintendo titles on the docket and no local authors on the roster. I couldn't help believing I could leverage my proximity to Nintendo's offices—and the savings on airfare and hotel costs—into an annual contract. And the abundance of biotech companies in the Seattle area meant plenty of opportunities for my wife. We talked for hours every night, time zones be damned, and by the time I finished the guide to *Eternal Darkness*, she had submitted her resignation.

Of course, I was only kidding about not coming home, but I did have somewhere else to go first.

I flew directly from Seattle to Los Angeles to attend the E3 onference, an event I soon realized existed solely to test the human ody's ability to live within a pinball machine. There is no preparing for he assault. Explosive sound effects and pop music rattle your brain, while a kaleidoscope of strobe lights leaves you seeing spots. But espite the migraine simulation, I pushed deeper into the convention enter, surfing an odorous wave of unwashed masses, in search of the nythical Demo Without a Line. It was enough to make this E3 virgin ppreciate the comparative boredom of trade show booth duty.

Two exhausting days later, following an overpriced lunch eaten while mercifully sitting on a reasonably clean patch of tile floor, I met with Leigh Davis. It was my first time seeing anyone from BradyGames in a year, and I couldn't wait to make my pitch. She offered me my first ontract thirty minutes later. It was a five-book, six-month deal that would pay $6500 per title. That initial contract would grow throughout he ensuing decade, eventually settling at nine books per year, for a otal that tickled six figures.[17]

---

[17] As games grew in complexity and the resulting strategy guides allooned in size, multiple payments would often be assigned to a single project. The *Diablo III* strategy guide, for example, required so many ewrites due to delays and an ever-changing skills system that no fewer han five of these monthly "book" payments were assigned to it over the span of my 2011 and 2012 contracts. I returned in 2013 to update the ook for the console port, then again in early 2014 for the *Reaper of Souls* expansion. By the time it was done, I had earned more than $80,000 writing the various guides for *Diablo III*. As Tim Bogenn used to say, it beat digging ditches.

And I'd need every dollar of it to live comfortably in the Seattle area.

My wife and I moved a month later, towing a jam-packed U-Haul across twelve states, ignorantly pushing our Isuzu beyond its towing capacity as we struggled over the Rockies at fifteen miles per hour with the pedal on the floor. The trip took three days plus a weekend I spent in Colorado training at elevation on the course for what should have been the world's first off-road Ironman-distance triathlon. The race was canceled a week later due to wildfires. Eight months of training and professional coaching literally gone up in smoke. This, like my bicycle crash two years prior, proved serendipitous, as I had barely finished unpacking my office before being called upon to help Tim wrap up the guide to *Super Mario Sunshine*. It was the last time he and I ever worked together.

BradyGames had over a dozen freelancers on call, but Tim and I would soon be the only two under contract. And with each of us often assigned to lead the effort for the year's biggest releases, it was only natural for our paths to diverge.[18] Though we seldom saw each other in the ensuing years (my move across the country certainly didn't help), I

---

[18] Tim and I would run into each other at E3 over the ensuing years and were always friendly with one another, but it wouldn't be until 2016, when I was at 2K Marin, updating the screenshots for the *Bioshock Collection* book, that we really got to spend time together. He was working on the guide for *Mafia III* with the affable Rick Barba, and the three of us had a few meals—and a lot of drinks—together. For as small a community as the strategy guide business was, it was a real shame our paths didn't cross more often.

never forgot that it was he who first introduced me to BradyGames. As it turned out, my story wasn't all that unique. Every strategy guide author I worked with over the years had been introduced to the business by someone already doing it. And each of us, in turn, paid it forward. Once.

The recipient of my karmic debt was Michael Lummis, a writer whose fantastically concise yet terribly unauthorized *Civilization III* e-guide, for sale on my long-defunct website, earned me a cease-and-desist from Random House. Michael would spend the ensuing decade spearheading the many strategy guides for *World of Warcraft*.

Better him than me.

Despite having worked in the industry for two years and been to Nintendo's headquarters for four prior projects, *Super Mario Sunshine* was the first proper Mario game I'd played since the days of the NES. Sadly, all I remember of the game, apart from the tropical theme and anthropomorphic water cannon Mario wore on his back, is an exhausting four days spent finding, describing, and mapping every one of the game's 240 Blue Coins. That it would count as a full book toward my contract was all the proof I needed that the move would pay off.

With *Super Mario Sunshine* done, along with several other titles that kept me busy through my first summer in the Pacific Northwest, I was soon summoned back to Nintendo to write the guide for *Star Fox Adventures.* The game cast second-tier mascot, Fox McCloud, in some heavily *Zelda*-inspired gameplay on Dinosaur Planet. Setting the game apart, however, was the periodic shift to the space combat sequences fans expected from prior *Star Fox* games.

And that's where things went awry.

Of the hundred-plus strategy guides I've written, my guide to *Star Fox Adventures* is the only one bearing a note that warns: "Due to the ongoing development of the game prior to the game release, there may be some slight differences between the screen shots shown in this guide and what appears in the game." And that would have been true, maddeningly so, if the chapter causing all the problems actually appeared in the book.

As popularized in the *Legend of Zelda* series, Fox McCloud's health meter consisted of a series of hearts that grew from three to seven over the course of the adventure. In the game build made available to me, this worked fine up until the final space combat sequence aboard Fox's Arwing spacecraft. That's when a bug appeared, limiting the Arwing's durability to three hearts. It was the most difficult part of the game, the final battle against archnemesis Andross, and the game had errantly reset the health meter to its initial state. Of course, I didn't know this was a bug.[19] I just thought the developers decided to make the climax damn near impossible.

For two consecutive days, I beat my head against the wall of that final battle, piloting my Arwing through the last space level in effort

---

[19] First- and second-party Nintendo titles were generally the most polished, stable pieces of software we ever encountered. Though we would generally receive no documentation or developer support, the fact that we could always rely on the game being essentially release quality made a big difference. This *Star Fox Adventures* (developed by Rare) bug was the only time I can recall encountering a major flaw in a game while on-site at Nintendo.

o reach Andross with the bulk of my three health hearts intact. I had no idea that I should have had twice as much health. The situation grew so dire that BradyGames even flew screenshot editor and gaming wiz Michael Owen out from Indiana to help me defeat the final boss. And on that third day, after hours spent passing the controller back and forth, I finally managed to defeat Andross despite having only half the health I should have had.

With the deadline looming, I stayed up all night, breaking down the video footage, analyzing every one of Andross's attacks, and writing one of the most detailed boss battle chapters I ever assembled. Then, as my wife's alarm clock broke the pre-dawn silence of the house, I uploaded the text and screenshots to the FTP server and went to bed.

My box of author's copies arrived a month later with my coverage of the final Andross battle nowhere to be found. Three days spent struggling with one of the toughest boss sequences I'd ever encounter, and nothing to show for it.

Though I knew standard practice was to always email the text files and use the FTP for screenshots, it never occurred to me that an editor wouldn't also check the FTP for documents. Nor did I think a check wouldn't be made to ensure each of the chapters in the table of contents was accounted for. Fingers were pointed and blame passed like a hot potato, eventually settling on my sleep-deprived failure to properly email the chapter. Fortunately, the readers didn't seem to mind, given that a full complement of seven hearts made the battle quite easy. Some even commented that they appreciated our book not spoiling the ending. Go figure.

Nevertheless, it was a mistake we could ill afford, as this was a period when as many as four strategy guides were published for every major GameCube release. BradyGames made the uncomfortable decision to undercut the competition by pricing our guides at $9.99, compared to the standard $12.99 of the time, but it was no less awkward for the writers. No longer willing to tie up multiple conference rooms for weeks at a time with teams of strategy guide authors, Nintendo moved a number of cubicles into a windowless storage room and shoved us in.

Those of us working for BradyGames were in one cubicle, a team working for Prima Games was steps away in another, and the guys writing for Versus were in an adjacent one; Nintendo's in-house *Player's Guides* were assembled elsewhere in the building. Given the screwup with *Star Fox Adventures* and the abundance of close-quarters competition, I was determined to knock it out of the park for *Metroid Prime*, one of the most anticipated games of the year and the eventual winner of multiple Game of the Year awards.

Sadly, that wasn't meant to be.

Despite everyone's efforts to speak in hushed tones and angle their monitors away from the aisle that split the room, lest rival authors discover that you, too, knew how to defeat the Omega Pirate, the truth was we were all essentially writing the same book. That was, until my co-

uthor decided not to wait around for access to *Metroid Fusion*, the
ompanion game for Game Boy Advance.

Each company intended to cover both games in a two-for-one
ombo book. Our plan was for me to spend the two weeks on-site writing
he bulk of the guide for *Metroid Prime* while my co-author covered the
nemies and in-game lore. Then, once Nintendo made the GBA
evelopment kits available, he would shift his attention to the smaller
Metroid Fusion. I'd help out if time permitted. But when Nintendo
urprised us by providing the in-game lore and enemy summaries on a
preadsheet, necessitating little more than copy and paste, he decided
o fly home rather than wait around to access *Metroid Fusion*—and
elping with *Metroid Prime* held no interest for him.

It wasn't until I got a phone call weeks later from a furious Leigh
Davis, demanding to know why *I* failed to cover *Metroid Fusion* that I
ealized I'd been thrown under the bus. Fortunately, unlike the conflict-
verse project editor who pleaded ignorance, I have no problem
defending myself when necessary. The book shipped with a single page
of *Metroid Fusion* coverage, not enough to warrant mention on the
over, my so-called co-author never wrote another strategy guide, and I
earned to personally make sure every aspect of a project was
accounted for, no matter how experienced the co-author or editor was.[20]

---

[20] Fortunately, all but one of my co-authors over the ensuing years
believed in continuing to help until the book was done. While it was
often beneficial to delineate roles (or at least assign chapters to one
another) early in the project, most were professional enough to take on
extra chapters if they finished up early.

My run through the 2002 GameCube hit parade hadn't gone as well as I had hoped, but my contract was renewed for a full ten books for 2003, and a big chance to redeem myself was scheduled to release that March.

No matter how many years pass or how many books I write, my strategy guide for *The Legend of Zelda: The Wind Waker* will always be among my favorites—and *Wind Waker* my favorite *Zelda* game. From the timeless cel-shaded graphics to the childish wonder of young Link heading out to explore a world of islands and sunken treasure, there was a joyfulness to the game that few others could rival. And best of all, I had time to do the guide right.

I spent the winter making my way through an imported copy of the Japanese release, taking notes, writing a draft of the walkthrough, and getting as familiar as I could with the game despite the language barrier. Then, when finally granted access to the North American release, I had three full weeks on-site to polish what would be my largest book to date.

The BradyGames guide for *The Legend of Zelda: The Wind Waker* was one of the first in the company's "Signature Series" line of books. Complete with a gold foil logo, 272 individually designed pages, and a fold-out poster of the entire 7x7 oceanic map, the book really was a terrific product.[21] Much of the credit is due to Alex Garner, the book's

---

[21] Producing a strategy guide of more than 160 pages at the time was a big deal. Little did we know we would soon struggle to keep the page count below 300 pages. Of all the strategy guides I'd work on, the

cartographer. Working from dozens of VHS tapes of my gameplay, Alex recreated over one hundred of the game's islands, temples, and caves in 3D, effectively rebuilding the entire world in a 3D modeling program. It was a Herculean effort, but one he wasn't keen on repeating ever again.

The success of the book left me feeling redeemed after the problems that plagued the *Star Fox Adventures* and *Metroid Prime* books. Unfortunately, Nintendo made the decision that summer to cease licensing their games for third-party strategy guides. Instead, *Nintendo Power's* various *Player's Guides* would have exclusive access going forward. It wasn't until the Nintendo Switch released fourteen years later, following the magazine's closure, that I'd be back on-site to write a guide for a first-party Nintendo title.

---

largest for a single game was the Legendary Edition of the guide for *Halo: Reach* at 480 pages, a full team effort. The *Bioshock Collection* guide, which covers all three games and all of the expansions and downloadable content weighed in at 560 pages.

Typecast McTwist

My leg shook as kids one third my age and half my height grew impatient around me. Despite knee pads and helmet armoring me against serious injury, I stood certain the only possible outcome involved paralysis and a headline that read: *Local Man Wins 2002 Darwin Award, Proves PlayStation Game Not Realistic*.

I extended the skateboard outward, bumping the wheels over the coping, and stomped my left foot down atop the tail, transforming the board into a plank. *Sink or swim*. Holding my breath, I shifted my right foot into position, leaned forward, and made the drop. An instant later I was zooming across the flat bottom of an eight-foot half-pipe, a little wobbly but upright. *What now?* I had no idea. I hadn't ridden a skateboard since the eighties, and even then only street, never vert. I surfed and would occasionally go snowboarding, so my balance was decent, but damn was that transition coming up fast. I'd love to say I effortlessly leaned into a backside railslide or wowed the kids with a crooked grind, but the real world has no Triangle Button.

The far side of the ramp offered no resistance. Momentum carried me up, straight up and out of the half-pipe. Then gravity took over. My skateboard and I separated. As I fell backward, eventually slamming the plywood decking, the board sailed ever higher into the air, accelerating as it flew past the platform atop the ramp, over the safety railing, and into the parking lot beyond the fence.

It was the worst crash I'd suffered since the accident that led to my career writing video game strategy guides. Little did I know back in 2000, as I based my writing sample on *Tony Hawk's Pro Skater,* that I'd end up authoring the guides for the bulk of the series going forward. That doing so wouldn't awaken my dormant skating skills was painfully unfortunate.

One of the benefits that came with writing unofficial guides for websites like IGN and Gamespy was the freedom to be snarky—always a winning play on the Internet—or even downright critical of a game or its features. This approach wasn't welcome over on the official side of the business, where strategy guide publishers paid big bucks for exclusive access to games but had to get the licensor's approval prior to publishing.[22]

---

[22] We had to refrain from criticizing individual skills or weapons within a game, too. It was fine to mention that a magic spell or weapon lacked damage in most situations, but we always had to find at least something positive to say, at least in the peripheral chapters. Similarly, we had to avoid always recommending the same weapon or skill, as it likely meant

It's fair to say that landing one of these authoring gigs was as much about connections and luck as it was ability, but not everyone managed to stick around. More than a few authors went AWOL in the middle of a project, proved too difficult to work with, or, in an extreme case involving the sequel to a fighting game, re-submitted the text from the prior game's guide. The ruse tricked the unsuspecting editor, but not the licensor.

I happened to submit my writing sample to BradyGames in 2000 just as the editor of the in-progress guide for *THPS2* was pulling his hair out over the state of the project. As it was explained to me later, the author for the *THPS2* guide had a habit of ridiculing the reader within the text he was turning in, stating that if a particular strategy didn't work, it was because the reader sucked at games.

I applaud his verve, and no doubt wish I could have written a few lines like that myself over the years—especially after reading some of the reviews left online—but antagonizing the player is rarely a good idea, and his mistake was my gain. The editor overseeing the guides for Activision's expanding line of action sports titles was more than ready to assign the upcoming books to me.

As stressful as it was to see the online projects dry up in 2001, it may have proved a blessing in disguise, as I was able to get out before

---

the game was unbalanced or that there was an overpowered weapon in the game. To have such stated in the strategy guide would be seen as the game publisher acknowledging the imbalance.

eveloping any bad habits. And just in time to skitch the coattails of the

urging X-Games popularity.

* * *

Greenville, North Carolina was the epicenter of the BMX world in the

early aughts. You couldn't swing an IGA sack without hitting someone

who'd won an X-Games medal. Naturally, the local presence of Dave

Mira, Ryan Nyquist, and their Mountain Dew entourages didn't actually

affect me. They weren't dropping by the Thursday night group rides at

the Bicycle Post to teach us roadies and tri-geeks how to do tailspins.

But that didn't stop me from name-checking their geographic proximity

as a reason why *I* was the right person to author the guide to *Mat

Hoffman's Pro BMX* in 2001, the first in a comically long line of spin-offs

and sequels to the Tony Hawk games. That my brother managed a

bicycle shop in New Jersey was equally irrelevant, yet that fact too made

it into my argument. I can only imagine the levels of eye rolling taking

place as the editors at BradyGames read my email.

Nevertheless, it worked.

Mat Hoffman's Pro BMX became my first-ever solo project for

BradyGames. It went well insofar as I managed to clear the bar of not

insulting the reader. And with that, Activision's burgeoning "O2" line of

action sports titles was effectively mine.[23] Later that year, a few months

---

[23] Technically, the Tony Hawk series of games existed largely outside the
"O2" label, as only *THPS3* and *THPS4* carry the logo of the short-lived

after flying to Indianapolis for my first face-to-face meeting with the BradyGames staff, I was back in their offices writing the guides to no fewer than three Tony Hawk games simultaneously. There was the hotly anticipated *Tony Hawk's Pro Skater 3* for the PlayStation 2, a scaled-down version bearing the same name for the original PlayStation, and Treyarch's terrific port, *Tony Hawk's Pro Skater 2X,* for Microsoft's new Xbox console. Later that month, I began writing the guide to *Shaun Palmer's Pro Snowboarder* the same day I wrapped up work on *THPS3*.

In a span of two years I'd gone from abusing the hell out of a Pizza Hut demo disc to enjoying exclusive early access to what would become many fans' favorite installment in one of the most popular franchises on the planet.[24] Some people never realize how good they have it. That's not how I'm wired. Women I'd meet would tell me how much their son would love to have my job. I countered by telling them their *husbands* wished they had my job.[25] And I believed this. I woke every day paranoid that would be the day it all ended, convinced the surging popularity of video games was creating an army of people looking to steal my job. So, I hustled, saying yes to every project I was

---

branding. Of the non-skateboarding games in the O2 lineup, only *Mat Hoffman's Pro BMX* ever received a sequel.

[24] Those who hold this opinion are wrong. *Tony Hawk's Pro Skater 4* is better. Fight me.

[25] Not once did I ever hear a mother say writing strategy guides would be interesting to her daughter. I suspect that would have changed going forward, if the business was still alive in the future, thanks to the greater number of women playing games now.

offered (with a few exceptions), even if it meant writing multiple books at once. [26]

What made it possible to work on so many of these guides simultaneously is what also led to me being typecast as the extreme sports guy. Regardless the sport—skateboarding, BMX, snowboarding, etc.,—these games were all more or less the same. Putting a guide together for a Tony Hawk or Mat Hoffman game was like following a recipe for a pasta dinner. No matter the shape of the noodle or the style of sauce, it's essentially the same thing. This isn't to say it was easy. We all know someone who can't help but serve mushy spaghetti.

BradyGames trusted me to get it *al dente* every time.

Each game had its cast of professional athletes, various pieces of branded equipment to provide cosmetic variety, and a dozen or so levels with a number of collectibles and scoring requirements. Completing the level objectives was seldom difficult, which meant anyone could "beat" one of these games with little trouble. But what drove players to buy the guidebooks—and caused the thumb muscles of

---

[26] There weren't many genres that I ever had to say no to. It was well-known that I wasn't the right guy for any games in the real-time strategy or fighting genres, but other than that, the only games I can remember turning down were *Call of Duty*, *Resident Evil*, and *Devil May Cry*. It wasn't because I didn't like those games—I've bought entries in each series—but because there were always games I was more interested in. That said, the topic of the then-upcoming *World of Warcraft* beta came up during a BradyGames author conference. I couldn't push back from the table fast enough.

my right hand to swell in size—was the hundreds of "gaps" scattered throughout the levels.

A gap is slang for an air or grind that incorporates pieces of terrain. In the real world, this translates to leaping between two adjacent ramps or jumping down a particular staircase. In the video game world, this could mean anything from airing off a rooftop into a concrete pool or grinding a series of power lines across town. Every gap had a name and awarded a point bonus. Working a few gaps into a combination would net you a higher score, but gaps were more about creativity. They were breadcrumbs hidden by the developers, designed to lead the player into the realm of outrageousness. My job was to reveal them.

People are often shocked to learn that strategy guide authors (usually) had to figure everything out on their own. One of the realities of modern game design, especially for AAA titles, is that each of the employees is hyper-focused on a singular aspect of the game, and very few in a development studio understand how the entire game comes together. They each have intimate knowledge of a single level or weapon. Or tree textures. But the whole game? They'll see it when it releases. I'll never forget being told by an executive at Gearbox Software that, when it came time to begin work on *Borderlands 2*, the first thing the team did was reach for our guide to the original game. It was the only piece of documentation they had that explained the entire game.

This is to say that the tactics and data you see compiled in a strategy guide were assembled by the author. Most often by playing it, testing hit-point damage, recording video, and manually going frame by ame to understand character animations, firing rates, jumping distances, etc.

Neversoft Entertainment, creators of the *Tony Hawk's Pro Skater* series, was one of the few exceptions. What began as a very simple game in 1999 had become exceedingly complex by the time the series wrapped up with its ninth installment, *Tony Hawk's Proving Ground*. Kevin Mulhall, my direct contact at Neversoft, understood how critical having accurate trick data would be to the guides. Rather than say it wasn't available or he didn't have time to compile it, he simply emailed me the files containing the scripts that governed the ever-expanding trick system. He trusted me with their special sauce, making it possible to cover all of the modifiers and variants, and ensure accurate point values for each. It would have been impossible otherwise.

Kevin was also quick to help me track down any gaps I couldn't find. Usually, the in-game gap checklist was all I needed. Many of their names were descriptive, like *THPS4*'s "Skylight-2-Skylight" gap on the Alcatraz level, but a few sometimes escaped my detection even after dozens of hours skating a single level. Strategy guide authors are rarely given direct access to someone at the studio—the Nintendos and Ubisofts of the world preferred to keep a wall between us—but Neversoft couldn't be bothered with such inefficiencies. If I was desperate for help,

I only needed to email Kevin and he'd answer with an illustrated screenshot, often within a day's time.[27]

Still, the gaps were what I stressed about most, even with the studio's help. I'd love to say our books were never wrong, but the Internet would eagerly prove this a lie. Though I did personally trigger every gap in each one of those games, errors occasionally made it to print. Sometimes a gap would change between the book being approved and the game's release. Other times, one of the numbered map callouts would get shifted during layout. And I'm sure I fell prey to a buggy gap triggering when it shouldn't have.

This isn't to say an omission was never my fault. Though competitive by nature, I've always approached games and contests with an eye toward the so-called spirit of the rules. Or, as far as video games are concerned, I played them as I believed the developers intended.[28] I'm not the type of gamer who looks for exploits or tries to "break the game" as I often hear said. My default path through a game mimics the elegant, graceful motion of a longboard surfer confined to the face of a

---

[27] Not only was this level of support unique, Kevin would also arrange for me to join their online multiplayer sessions remotely while *THPS4* was in development. What a treat it was to play online in the PS2 era with Joel Jewett, head of Neversoft, Kevin, and many of the other devs. Though I did eventually burn out on the series, like everyone did, I'll forever appreciate Neversoft including me in the end credits for *THPS4*. The "Special Thanks" were truly all mine to give.
[28] Of course, who's to say what a team of dozens (or hundreds) intended?

ave, as opposed to the choppy, aggressive stylings of a short-boarder
eeking to launch beyond the curl.

And this is why the popular "shuffle" technique in *Tony Hawk's*
ro Skater never occurred to me. The player's ultimate goal was to score
oints by amassing lengthy trick combos. The more tricks you perform,
he higher the multiplier. Though I obviously aimed to build my combo as
igh as I could, I never knew just how fast a player could trick in and out
f grinds. That is, until someone noticed my screen name while playing
ony Hawk's Pro Skater 4* online with the PlayStation 2 and promptly
alled me out for my failure to mention it. According to him (safe bet that
. was a male), the entire guide was shit because I didn't explain the
huffle technique.[29]

I learned two things that day. First, and most importantly, was
ever to share my online alias in a public space. And second, to always
sk the testers if they had any favorite tricks or exploits that I should

---

[9] Exploits like this existed in a lot of games, but it was always unclear
whether or not the game publishers wanted them discussed. This even
extended to overpowered weapons or skills. One game studio pushed
back against my frequent recommendations to use a particular fire
attack, as they wanted to encourage players to use the other elements.
Unfortunately, the others weren't nearly as effective as the unbalanced
fire attack. Surprisingly, gamers themselves would sometimes complain
about a guide that emphasized a single skill too often, as was the case
with the *Final Fantasy VII: Crisis Core* guide I wrote with Joe Epstein. The
game featured a skill called Costly Punch that was so overpowering, so
wonderfully effective, that you'd be silly not to use it. To play the game
without using Costly Punch would be like playing as the Raiders in
Tecmo Bowl and never handing off to Bo Jackson.

know about. I included a note about the shuffle technique in the guide for *Tony Hawk's Underground* and every book that followed.

I wound up authoring thirteen board-and-bike strategy guides before Neversoft shifted focus to *Guitar Hero* and Activision realized the mule they'd been flogging died years earlier. My passion for those projects, despite being briefly rekindled with *Tony Hawk's Proving Ground,* had flickered out after the first few guides, but they'll always hold a special place in my heart. Not only did the preponderance of Tony Hawk sequels grant me an opportunity to prove myself to BradyGames, but they also got me an invite to my first E3 party.

* * *

"I need something to wear to a Hollywood party."

The saleswoman shot me a look that said I might as well have asked her to repair my flux capacitor. "You know this is Carolina East Mall, right?" She clucked. "Do I look like I know what people wear in Hollywood?"

No, she did not. But I was desperate. And a touch nerdy. Again. But this was the world I inhabited; the pinched corridor between the Venn ballrooms of geeks and jocks.

I bought a pair of baggy but classy black pants from some nineties brand like Stussy or Mossimo and a blue short-sleeve button-down that looked like silk, but felt like, well ... *felt*. The shirt was by Quiksilver. I point this out not because I expect anyone to be impressed, but because then six-time world champion—and Quiksilver athlete—Kelly Slater was also on the guest list.

The invitation arrived in a halved tennis ball can bearing the Activision O2 logo. It was the summer of 2002 and not only was I headed to my first E3 conference, but I was also invited to attend a party at Paramount Studios. A "house party" at a Hollywood sound stage. Why a tennis ball can, I have no idea. Maybe they knew I needed a pen caddy for my desk?

At the conference, I stood in line with a stack of my books, excited to get them signed by the athletes gracing the covers: Tony Hawk, Mat Hoffman, Kelly Slater, and Shaun Palmer. Hawk was a no-show and Palmer refused to sign anything but the sponsor-provided poster, but Hoffman and Slater were very cool, each taking a moment to talk about the guides. Shaun Murray, a pro wakeboarder, occupied the last seat at the table, but we didn't do a guide for his game, so ... *awkward*.

That night, me and a few of the business folks from BradyGames made our way to the Paramount lot and were pointed to a soundstage where the party was held. Shaun Palmer, clad in a sweaty tank top and looking as if he had just wrestled a snowman, pushed past in a huff, anxious to leave. Hawk didn't show and I never spotted Slater either, but Hoffman was there. As was a not-quite-sixteen-year-old Shaun White, holding court with a gaggle of pretty young girls.[30] And

---

[30] What's with all these guys being named Shaun?

that's as close as I came to the guy who'd go on to become the greatest X-Games and Olympic snowboarder of all time.

I wandered the party alone, ducking in and out of various rooms decorated to match each of the sports games. The band wasn't impressive, my feet were dead tired from a day on the show floor, and I wasn't much for mingling. I needed to find a place to sit. Instead, I found a solitary Mat Hoffman. He was slouched in a chair in a snowboarding-themed playroom, a DualShock 2 in hand, a couple of drinks beside him, staring at the television as the PS2 went through its boot sequence. The title screen for *Shaun Palmer's Pro Snowboarder* appeared and Mat sighed a cloud of alcohol. "The Condor" rose and took a giant stride across the room, hit the console's reset button, and returned to his seat.

The boot sequence repeated. The logo for Palmer's game appeared again, and Mat let out a mournful wale. I asked him what was wrong, unsure if he even knew I was there, and doubting he'd remember me from earlier in the day.

"I want to play *my* game," he said, and again stood and hit the reset button. He flopped back into the chair, kicking aside an empty Solo cup, his eyes locked on the screen.

"Come with me," I said, "Your game's in another room."

"I want to play *my* game," he repeated and dropped the controller.

I want to say we made our way to the BMX room and that I literally beat Mat Hoffman at his own game. It would have been easy, I'm sure, as I had recently finished writing the guide for *Mat Hoffman's Pro*

BMX 2. Also, I was sober. But the truth is Mat never followed me. He never noticed I was there. Instead, he simply hit the reset button a third time and took his seat yet again, ever hopeful his game would magically appear on the television.

Enter the Mediocrity

Gamers of a certain age are undoubtedly familiar with the dubious history that movie tie-ins have enjoyed over the years. Those who grew up with the Atari 2600 no doubt recall the pixelated outline of a U-shaped trench, a telescopic neck, and the controller-throwing rage of a beige alien named E.T. falling in said pit over and over. And over. Thousands of unsold *E.T. the Extra Terrestrial* game cartridges were famously plowed into a similar hole months later. The bulk of the gaming industry followed soon after, resulting in the video game crash of 1983.

Video games have enjoyed a pretty good run since the NES reached worldwide success several years later, but discerning gamers still know to give movie tie-ins a wide berth until the reviews are in. Though there have been a few very good tie-in games over the years—I had the pleasure of writing the guides to *Spider-Man 2* and the criminally under-appreciated *Tron 2.0*—the industry is littered with games emitting the stench of a cash grab. From the *Top Gun* and *Back* o the Future foibles of the NES generation to the more recent disaster that was Aliens: Colonial Marines, the examples are numerous. But the ault is not always so clear, as there can be a number of valid reasons or the critical failure of these titles.

Often, as was the case with E.T. the Extra Terrestrial, it's a matter of limited time and personnel, as money that could be spent on development gets gobbled up like so many Reese's Pieces by licensing ees and marketing expenditures. Worse still is the tendency to rush the game's development in order to release alongside the movie—or in time for Christmas.[31] Other times, the reasons for a game's failure to live up to the movie stem from a more cynical aspect of human nature: belief that the sheer popularity of the movie franchise is enough to guarantee sales. This is especially true for games targeted at younger players, commonly bought by undiscerning parents. For example, the various Shrek games are notoriously inferior to the movies upon which they're based. But perhaps for good reason. Unlike the well-received LEGO games, which were largely based on decades-old movie franchises, the Shrek games primarily released within months of the corresponding movie, whether they were finished or not.

I received most of my assignments by email, often going a full year with only one or two phones calls to my editor-in-chief. To receive a call from her boss, the head of the imprint, was unheard of for a new author. Though I always had the option to decline a project if it didn't

---

[31] E.T. was famously made by a single person, Howard Scott Warshaw, in just over five weeks.

match my tastes—I rage-uninstalled the beta for *Overwatch* in 2016 and begged off the project in less than an hour—saying no to a personal request from the publisher wasn't, shall we say, a strong career move.[32]

Even in 2010, with more than seventy guidebooks under my belt, I knew to set aside my personal taste in games when the publisher came calling. One minute I was a proud contrarian, content in my *Halo*-free existence, then a few short moments later I was agreeing to write the single-player campaign for *Halo: Reach*. And though the project took me two full months to complete, most of it on-site at 343 Industries, I was glad I said yes. *Halo: Reach* went on to become one of my favorite games of the Xbox 360 generation, with many critics proclaiming it the best of the franchise. Of course, *Halo: Reach* had been in development for nearly three years with no Hollywood schedule to abide.

The same cannot be said about the subject of a phone call I received back in 2003, months into my first ten-book contract. David Waybright, then head of BradyGames, was practically vibrating with excitement over the game they had secured. It was one of their biggest licensing deals to date; it would be their most important book of the year; I had to swear myself to secrecy, promising not to reveal even a detail to my wife. I was intrigued, for sure, and quite flattered that I was the one getting the call.

---

[32] Blizzard ultimately declined to pursue a strategy guide for *Overwatch*. While I wanted to believe it was because they anticipated how much post-release balancing and additions there would be, I couldn't help viewing this as an early indicator that the strategy guide industry was rapidly approaching its expiration date.

My young ego would have agreed to anything at that point.

The game was *Enter the Matrix*, arguably the biggest movie tie-in of all time. The game would release alongside the long-awaited sequel to one of the nineties' top films. It also contained a full hour of exclusive movie footage filmed by the famed Wachowski Brothers. The only way to get the complete experience of *The Matrix Reloaded* would be to play through its companion game, *Enter the Matrix*.

Not only would I be among the first to play the game, a normal occurrence for strategy guide authors, but not even the development team had seen the movie footage. Top secret indeed.

* * *

The first two days on-site are never productive. Without fail, someone either forgets to reserve the conference room, the game build doesn't work, a power cord has gone missing, or our contact calls out sick. Entire days have passed in corporate lobbies, flipping through years-old gaming magazines, trying to ignore the sizzle reel eternally looping on the ever-present television.

That's how it normally goes. My introduction to Shiny Entertainment, the long-defunct *Enter the Matrix* developer, was quite different. Rather than waiting around for an associate producer to retrieve me, I was quickly met by David Perry, the slick-dressed founder of the studio.

Perry built a name for himself in the nineties with smash hits *Earthworm Jim* for the Sega Genesis and *MDK* for the PC and PlayStation. Their more recent release, *Sacrifice,* was among their most critically-praised titles. As an avid R.E.M. fan, I was keen to ask if it was true that he named the studio after the band's most annoying song, "Shiny Happy People." Unfortunately, Perry's demeanor made it clear he wasn't there for idle chat.

Underscoring the sensitivity surrounding the promised hour of exclusive *Matrix Reloaded* footage contained within the game, Perry wasted little time confirming I had signed the necessary non-disclosure agreements. I had. He then drew himself up to his full six-foot-something height and said, "If you breathe a word about this footage to anyone, your body will wash up on a beach."

It's funny how the human mind works when your integrity is questioned. Up until then I hadn't told anyone I'd be writing the game's guidebook, and I certainly had no intention of even mentioning the movie footage to my wife. But Perry's smug, wannabe tough-guy approach made me laugh. And as I stood there chuckling, trying to lighten the mood, I couldn't help wondering what *The Hollywood Reporter* would pay for a scoop.

Not that I ever said a word. The honest truth is, other than signaling an early thumbs-up or down to a friend, I never once considered leaking details about a project. Where was the incentive? What could Kotaku or IGN possibly give to make it worth jeopardizing a gig that paid between ten and thirty thousand dollars per strategy guide?

omeone at Namco-Bandai once accused BradyGames authors of
aking a game's achievement data. While I'm sure being the
nonymous hero of the *Dragon Ball Z* community for a day is its own
eward, the notion of any of us risking our careers was absurd.

I mention the body-on-a-beach comment primarily for comedic
alue, but what Perry said a few minutes later, while ushering me to a
ecure room containing the game, was no laughing matter. Rather, it
vas quite the red flag.

Hopped up on the excitement of having somehow landed the
vhale of all movie tie-ins, Perry was ecstatic when it came to discussing
he movie footage. Filmed by the Wachowski Brothers in tandem with
he main movie, it was indistinguishable in terms of production values
and special effects. But Perry owned a game company. Surely, he was
hrilled about the game they were making, right? The one I was on hand
o document?

With no indication he was anything but absolutely serious, he
oragged, "We can wrap this footage around a *Tetris* clone and sell five-
million copies."

And just like that, before ever picking up a controller, I knew to
emper any excitement I had for the game.

My first two hours with an *Enter the Matrix* beta build were an
utter disappointment.[33] Though I knew Neo and Trinity weren't playable

---

[33] I actually walked outside after this play session to call Waybright at
BradyGames in attempt to warn him that the game was not good. I had
heard rumors that they had offered Shiny as much as one million dollars

in the game, there was no preparing for how uninteresting the replacement characters proved to be. Instead of Keanu Reeves and Carrie-Anne Moss, we got Will Smith's wife playing the role of—let me look this up—*Niobe?* Worse still, the combat system offered a mere fraction of the moves Perry promised in the run-up to the game's release.

While I doubt anyone took his hyperbolic claims of two thousand attack moves seriously, it was clear the figure was off by a factor of ten ... or eighty. The only way to avoid seeing the same repetitive dozen or so context-sensitive maneuvers was to contort Niobe and Ghost (Anthony Wong's character) into some unlikely positions. The animations were wonderfully done—Shiny spared no expense when it came to motion-capture—but the joy of stumbling onto a new attack was far too infrequent and unpredictable to keep the game fresh.

Still, it was the bugs that were most disconcerting. And it took only a few hours to realize the game wasn't ready to have a strategy guide written for it. I departed for home the next day, expecting the release date to be pushed back by months.

How naive of me.

---

in licensing fees for the project, and I had a feeling once word got out about the game, guidebooks sales would be nonexistent. Waybright seemed to appreciate the call, but, perhaps like Perry, he knew that the branding alone would be enough to sell the guide. Either way, the deal was signed. All we could do was make the best guide possible and hope the reviews didn't scare off too many sales.

I was ordered back to California two weeks later, this time to Warner Bros. studios in Burbank. Although an inexplicable swampy green filter continued to muddy the graphics—and my screenshots—there was no denying that development had progressed.

The controls were tighter, and many of the show-stopping bugs had been exterminated, making it possible to play through the game with Jada Pinkett Smith's character, Niobe. While the bullet-dodging "Focus" system earned the game generous comparisons to 2001's *Max Payne,* one couldn't ignore how empty *Enter the Matrix* felt.[34] Thumbing through the strategy guide today reveals hundreds of screenshots showcasing barren walls and furniture-free rooms. Momentary flourishes like a cascade of papers flying in the air did little to disguise the fact that the game was ultimately a lengthy sequence of vacant offices, sewers, and highways.

Yes, the highways. Video game developers share a rich history of shoehorning ill-advised driving sequences into action games, dating back at least to 1989's *The Adventures of Bayou Billy* on the NES. And while thirteen-year-old-me was free to throw a gamepad in the privacy of my basement, adult me, on-site at Warner Bros., needed to be on good behavior.

Alas, I'm only human.

---

[34] The bullet-dodging effect done so well in games like *Max Payne* and, later, *F.E.A.R.* was, in turn, inspired by *The Matrix* movies. That *Enter the Matrix* itself was ultimately the least successful of the three is an ironic coda to gaming's fascination with slow-motion "bullet time" effects.

Enter the Matrix is far from the only game that left me cursing mad, but it is the only one for which I had to buy the publisher a new DualShock 2. One particular driving sequence left me so frustrated that began twisting the controller in my hands as I grit my teeth, being caref not to unleash a verbal outburst in a crowded office. I continued twistin and grinding until the shoulder buttons suddenly popped loose and wer sailing over the cubicle divider, into someone's office. I tried not to mak eye contact as I retrieved the R2 button from the floor.

Despite the problems with the game, Enter the Matrix was an important title for BradyGames—and they were pulling out all the stops. Led by the company's resident fanboy, the design team was instructed to sprinkle hidden ciphers throughout the book for use in the game's hacking mode. We amassed images from the movie set, interviews with developers and actors, and a story timeline that went further down the rabbit hole than any previously published. The quality of the game was irrelevant. We all had a job to do, and that was to create the best strategy guide we could for a franchise we loved. Or previously did.

* * *

Enter the Matrix did go on to sell five million copies, as Perry predicted. Perhaps a Tetris clone would have had fewer returns. While I could find no public records, I distinctly recall retailer EB Games (formerly Electronics Boutique) discontinuing their policy of allowing video game returns in the summer of 2003, shortly after the game's May release.

Rumors at the time attributed the decision to *Enter the Matrix*, with some calling it the most returned video game of all time.

Apparently more people were ready to be unplugged than Morpheus thought.

Critics and the public were largely split on the title, with diehard fans opting to focus on the game's potential as opposed to its shortcomings. I suspect it was that wasted potential that led to the game ultimately scoring a lowly 62 on Metacritic. One reviewer, writing for *Electronic Gaming Monthly*, commented, "In more than 20 years of playing games, I have never seen a console game as obviously unfinished and rushed to market as *Enter the Matrix*."

As I type these words nearly sixteen years later, a single memory comes to mind. I was on-site at Shiny Entertainment, cramming to flesh out the chapters devoted to the game's hacking system a day or two before deadline. It was nearly three o'clock in the morning and I was one of a handful of people in the building. Suddenly, a developer I hadn't met approached. He looked as if he hadn't slept or showered in days. He was barefoot, his tee shirt's neckhole was stretched, and his hair looked electrocuted. He slumped against the wall, dragged a hand over his face, and said, "Just tell me the truth. Is it any good?"

I wanted to be honest. I wanted to tell him that it could be good only if they got out from under Hollywood's movie schedule and delayed the game by a year. I wanted to tell him *Enter the Matrix* would be good only if Shiny's leadership were as enthusiastic about the game as they were the exclusive movie footage. No, too much work still remained, I thought. The graphics needed to be overhauled, the driving segments stripped out, and the entire game remade starring Neo, Trinity, and Morpheus as playable characters.

But I chose to lie.

Whether or not he appreciated my mumbled banality about Ghost's combat skills being really cool didn't matter. He knew the truth. He wouldn't have asked otherwise.

The staff that made the game did their best—I have no doubt— but they were given an impossible task. Movie tie-ins were hard enough in the best circumstances. And the blurring lines between Hollywood and video games only made them harder—especially when Hollywood dictated the schedule. Maybe *Enter the Matrix* wouldn't have sold five million copies without the movie footage. Maybe it would have sold more had the studio possessed the time it needed to make a better game. Who can say?

What's clear is that our beloved hobby had hit an inflection point. It was always a business, true, but the early aughts ushered in an era in which the game would never again be enough. Movie footage, merchandising, pre-order bonuses, downloadable content, monthly subscriptions, microtransactions, and loot crates all built atop one another to create the games-as-service model so common today. Even strategy guides morphed from a simple softcover book sold at a reasonable price to slip-case exclusives packing all manner of flotsam to justify a price tag approaching one hundred dollars.

Shiny Entertainment got a second chance to do it right and released *The Matrix: Path of Neo* two years later, this time starring the famous Keanu Reeves character. But by then the damage was done. Though the game received a warmer critical reception, public interest in the franchise faded quickly after the second movie's release and Shiny Entertainment closed in 2007.

Oddly enough, *Enter the Matrix's* prized companion footage did little to help me better understand *The Matrix Reloaded's* convoluted plot. Nor did it leave me with any interest in seeing the trilogy's finale. To this day, I have never heard anyone mention *The Matrix Revolutions*, except as a punch line.

I don't deny that we strategy guide writers worked along the periphery of the gaming industry. Few of us truly knew what it was like to work in development. And, to be honest, much of our direct contact was with those on the licensing side of the business. But many of us spent countless days at myriad studios. In my eighteen years writing strategy guides, I spent time on-site at each of the following companies: 2K Games, 343 Studios, Blizzard, Bungie, Capcom USA, The Coalition, Epic Games, Gearbox Studios, Irrational Games, Konami, Microsoft, Nintendo of America, Platinum Games (Osaka), Shiny Entertainment, Square-Enix, and Warner Bros. (Montreal). I may even be forgetting a few.

During the weeks on-site at these companies, I couldn't help getting a feel for the culture and employee morale. It should come as no surprise to learn that these metrics seemed to rise directly with the quality of the game being developed—or at least the time allowed to create it. It also carried over to how our presence was regarded and the level of support we received. And, when it came to making us feel at home, one studio's level of hospitality was truly Epic.

R.I.P. Dom

For many fans, their earliest memory of *Gears of War* is of a solitary Marcus Fenix taking cover in a ruined alley while the hauntingly melodic *Donnie Darko* version of the song "Mad World" plays on. The trailer, released in the fall of 2006, was devoid of in-game sound effects, text, and voice-over. It was just Marcus running from the silhouetted spider-boss that would come to be known as the Corpser. The trailer's official YouTube upload has over twelve million views as of early 2019, no doubt catapulting Michael Andrews's and Gary Jules's cover of the song to far loftier heights than Tears for Fears ever dreamed. To hear the song and not think about *Gears of War* is impossible.

Yet, my first memory involving the game came several months earlier, at the 2006 E3 conference. Shortly before my arrival at the Los Angeles Convention Center, I had been told to make sure I got in to see this game called *Gears of War*. It was to be my big fall project. I can't say I was particularly excited. Knowing it was from the studio behind *Unreal*

Tournament left me lukewarm to the whole thing, as PC shooters weren't particularly my style.[35] Those *Daikatana* flashbacks were strong.

My disinterest evaporated as soon as I reached the BradyGames booth, where a twenty-foot-long wall was wrapped in a guns-ablaze *Gears of War* mural. I still knew nothing of the game, but knowing I'd be writing the guide for a title warranting that kind of splash left me walking around with my chest puffed out for days.

Anxious to see what the fuss was about, I made my way to the private theater where Epic Games was demonstrating *Gears of War*. Unfortunately, half the population of Los Angeles had the same idea. Humanity snaked as far as I could see, encircling the Microsoft booth, constricting traffic, swallowing hours of people's lives. One convention goer pegged the end of the line somewhere in the Mojave Desert.

I'm allergic to lines.

Worse, this wasn't Six Flags. Not only was there no Flash Pass to wave en route to the front of the line, I'm self-aware enough to know no form of "do you know who I am" would ever work for me. Especially not in Los Angeles. Least of all at a convention with Clint Eastwood, Robin Williams, and Paris Hilton milling about.

But I was desperate. And on the show's final day, moments before the last demo began, I approached the door of the at-capacity theater and introduced myself. I said I was from BradyGames and that

---

[35] I soon got over my aversion to first-person shooters and would end up writing the guides to numerous games in the genre, including the entire *Bioshock* trilogy, *Singularity*, *The Darkness II*, *Hour of Victory* (we which jokingly referred to as Hour of Gameplay), *DOOM*, and *Halo: Reach*.

'd be writing the guide for *Gears of War*, and that it was really important
 get in to see it. I was on the verge of groveling. I crossed my fingers,
hoping for a spot on the floor—even one in the back corner would have
been fine—but I expected my plea to be met with a roll of the eyes and
instructions to be on my way. I certainly didn't expect to be positioned
near the podium as studio exec Mark Rein demoed the game beside
me.

My apologies to any attendees who mistook me for one of the
studio's hotshot game designers.

Behind the movie screen, I spotted a closet filled with consoles,
monitors, and a technician. Whether Rein was demoing the game live or
controller-syncing his way through a Milli Vanilli-esque performance, I
couldn't tell. Nor did I care; the game looked fucking awesome.

Gears of War is a third-person shooter that melds an inventive
cover system and bleeding edge graphics with the most unapologetically
violent—and gory—gameplay of the Xbox 360 generation. Not until
2016's *DOOM* did another AAA game approach the combat's over-the-
top gratuitousness. Sure, plenty of games had muscle-bound "space
marines" with big guns, but only *Gears of War* gave you an assault rifle
with a chainsaw under the barrel. And when players tired of bisecting
enemies with uppercut chainsaw swings through the crotch, they were
free to curb stomp a downed foe, splattering their head across the
ground like roadkill.

But *Gears of War* wasn't all destroyed beauty and characters
admonishing one another to "walk it off, pussy." The game had heart. To

play the series was to fall in love with Delta Squad. If not the gruff protagonist, Marcus, or the wise-cracking Baird, then certainly Cole or Dom—or Kenny, err, I mean Carmine.[36] Additional characters would fill out the various squads over the ensuing years, but the original heroes of Delta Squad would never be forgotten.

I couldn't help laughing when I discovered Epic Games was located in North Carolina. How ironic, I thought, realizing that I'd moved to Washington to be closer to a company for which we no longer wrote guides, only to be sent back to North Carolina every other year to head up efforts on the various *Gears* books. But make no mistake; I loved my biennial trips to Epic Games.

With a keycode granting 24/7 access, an open invitation to the nightly catered dinners, and permission to join the daily multiplayer playtest sessions, Epic Games provided everything we needed to create the best guidebook we could. Rod Ferguson, the executive producer, even arranged one-on-one meetings with each of the level designers to ensure I didn't miss anything.[37] Finding the game's collectible COG Tags

---

[36] A running joke throughout the *Gears of War* series is that every game has a private Carmine (last name). In each of the games Carmine meets an untimely demise in somewhat comedic fashion, much like the *South Park* character, Kenny.

[37] I'd run into Rod every other year throughout the next decade, on-site at Epic throughout the *Gears of War* trilogy, at Irrational Games during his eight-month stint working on *Bioshock Infinite*, and then at The Coalition while writing the guide to *Gears of War 4*. The rise from producer to studio head couldn't have happened to a nicer guy.

as never hard, but the game was filled with subtle touches that needed
o be highlighted.

Despite the terrific support from the studio—and no
nterference from Microsoft—the project was still too large for a single
erson, especially given the game's emphasis on multiplayer. To that
nd, I managed to convince Leigh Davis to hire my friend Jim Morey to
ssist as a multiplayer consultant.

The poor guy had no idea what he was signing up for.

Other than the daily one-hour playtest sessions, Jim and I were
n our own to devise strategy for the eight-person multiplayer portion of
he game. The wonder of being on-site at Epic wore off quickly, and it
vasn't long before Jim was questioning the wisdom of taking a week's
vacation from work and family to spend fourteen hours a day
hotgunning bots in half. True, we spent much of the day playing the
oeta of what would become our favorite franchise of all time, but we
vere only too aware how futile it was to write tactical advice based on
wo-person matches.

There was no doubt the game would garner a sequel, and I
nated to think Jim might swear off ever helping me again. Fortunately,
he chance to rub elbows with one of gaming's biggest names was
enough to keep him coming back.

* * *

It is impossible to write about *Gears of War* without mentioning Cliff Bleszinsky, the creator and lead designer of the series. I first met Cliff in a playtest session, the morning of my first day on-site in 2006. I had barely played through the single-player campaign's opening scene before receiving one of the coveted slots in the 4v4 multiplayer session the studio ran each morning.

Playtest sessions served two purposes: the network staff could monitor performance, while various designers and programmers discussed weapon balancing and general gameplay. That said, competition was fierce, and having me on your team that day was a liability.

After routinely being one of the first players eliminated in each game, I somehow found my way to a one-on-one showdown against Cliff in the day's final match. We were playing Gridlock, what would become the game's most popular map, and Cliff was in the tower with the Boomshot, a rocket launcher equivalent. If there was one thing I had excelled at so far that day, it was catching Boomshot rockets in the face.

I poked my head out from behind the husk of a burned-out car and heard the telltale sound of the Boomshot firing. I dodge-rolled to the side in time, taking heavy damage but escaping death. "He's only got one shot left," one of my teammates called out. "He's on the left-hand stairs," another said, clearly screen-watching.

I circled around, sliding in and out of cover, praying I'd find a power weapon. I had no idea where the Frag Grenades spawned, nor did I know the Longshot (sniper rifle) I craved was in the tower with Cliff. I

as a total noob, running for cover, being hunted by the game's lead
esigner.

Cliff fired again, but the shot sailed overhead as I rolled toward
m. *Shit*, I thought, seeing his character right next to me. I panicked and
'essed the melee button, knocking him back, then hip-fired the
nasher, blasting Cliff's character into chunks with a move that would
ɔme to be known as the two-piece. And for those still judging the
egree of skill (or lack thereof) needed to employ this technique, allow
ıy story to be the closing argument.

The room erupted in laughter and jeers, and more than one
and slapped me on the back in congratulations. Cliff approached as we
'ere leaving the playtest room. He shook my hand and introduced
imself, as if he needed to, then said, "I guess we got the right guy
'riting the guide."

One of the great things about returning to Epic Games every
ther year was seeing how well the studio's employees seemed to be
aken care of. Between *Gears of War*'s success and the Unreal engine's
videspread licensing, Epic was awash in money. When we returned for
iears of War 3, their offices had seemingly tripled in size, with the new
ıddition containing a massive kitchen and eating area, complete with
ock climbing wall and a metal slide descending from the second floor.
)f course, staying true to the stereotypes of awkward, physically
ıncoordinated gamers, one employee apparently broke a leg on the
ılide. From that moment on, would-be sliders were required to sign a
vaiver before utilizing the playground equipment.

We really can't have nice things.

By then, our writing team had expanded to five: a squad of four assigned to multiplayer and yours truly handling the campaign. The new expansion couldn't have come at a better time. Instead of being crammed into a small, glass-encased conference room, aka "The Fishbowl," we were given the back section of their new, state-of-the-art playtest area, complete with more than twenty stations and an accordion-style partition that could wall off sections of the room for quiet. This proved particularly important when multiplayer assistant Kenny Sims took to hollering a battle cry with each bayonet charge.

Architectural improvements aside, the most interesting sign of the company's success sat outside. During my first trip, in 2006, the Epic Games parking lot was pretty standard. Barring an appearance from studio founder Tim Sweeney' Ferrari on a sunny day, it was your basic collection of sedans and compacts with an occasional Mustang or 350Z thrown in for good measure. A few additional sports cars were sprinkled in when we returned for the sequel, but little worth writing about. But two years later, when we were back on-site for *Gears of War 3*, one couldn't turn around without spotting an Audi R8, a Lotus, or Maserati. Porsches and Corvettes were as common as Honda Accords outside most other studios—especially those that don't manage to keep their company private.

Several of us sat outside a Subway sandwich shop one afternoon, taking a break from *Gears of War 3*, when the unmistakable growl of Cliff Bleszinski's Lamborghini caught our attention. Cliff pulled into the lot, parked alongside a minivan and hopped out. Not expecting him to remember us from prior visits in years past, we were surprised when he slid into the bench seating beside me.

He welcomed us back to the studio. Asked if we had everything we needed, how long we'd be on-site, and if we were enjoying the game. This wasn't the demeanor of a man "observing himself" as Tom Bissell wrote in his book, *Extra Lives*, but someone genuinely excited about his work—and his role as host.

When I told him we'd been there for a few days already, he quickly looked side to side, then leaned in and asked, "What'd you think of the scene?"

He must not have noticed our confused looks.

"We actually got in touch with Michael Andrews who did the *Donnie Darko* version of "Mad World" with Gary Jules, and had him record the instrumental that plays during Dom's death."

My co-authors and I stared at him with our mouths agape, eyes wide. I was the only one playing the campaign—the others were there for the multiplayer modes and had forbidden me from telling them anything about the plot—and I had only just reached the start of Act 3 before lunch.

Our shock was obvious and Cliff noticed. "Oh shit, I just spoiled the biggest secret in the game," he said, face-palming for effect.

I tried forgetting what I had heard as Cliff apologized. The factoid about the song was great; I couldn't wait to hear it. But Dom? Dom was going to die?

Cliff got up from the table, apologized again, and disappeared into the Subway. Jim looked across the table, shaking his head, and said, "Well, if you're gonna have one of the biggest reveals of the year spoiled for you, it might as well be by the creator of the franchise." I couldn't agree more, and my mind quickly looked ahead to the challenge of not spoiling the moment for readers of our book.

Later that evening, back on the planet of Sera, I reached a fuel depot in the town of Mercy, where Dizzy and Jace were pinned down. It was up to the player-character, Marcus, and his crew of Dom, Anya, and Samantha to hold off an endless stream of enemies until someone devised an escape plan. In the guide, the final sentence I wrote for this chapter reads: "Put the Gnasher's short-range stopping power to the test, and hold them off long enough for Dom to devise an escape plan."

What I didn't say was that Dom's plan was a suicide mission.

To this day, hearing even a few bars of Gary Jules's and Michael Andrews's version of "Mad World" gives me goose bumps. That evening, despite knowing that Dom would die at some point in the game, I cried. And, as Cliff no doubt intended, it was the excruciatingly slow instrumental by Michael Andrews that sent the tears streaming. I knew what was about to happen: Dom intended to crash the truck into the fuel depot and save his friends. More importantly, he was going to join his wife Maria in heaven.

This wasn't the first time I teared up playing a video game. The scene in *Okami* where Issun, the sprite, forcefully tells best friend Amaterasu, the wolf-character, that they must split up had me in tears as well. The sounds of Amaterasu's whimper, her sad, drooping stance, her constant efforts to follow Issun as he left were too much. They reminded me of my own dogs and the inevitable goodbye we'd have to endure when age and disease eventually struck.

Yet it was different with *Gears of War 3*. It wasn't a trick to pull on the heartstrings of dog lovers. Anyone can create a tearjerker by including a dying, lost, or abandoned canine. But few pieces of media, particularly one as unapologetically gory as *Gears*, can make people mourn the loss of a character. Especially a grown male character. And that was the beauty of *Gears of War*. In my opinion, no other shooter franchise has come close to telling as engrossing a story. From Marcus's complicated relationship with his father to Dom mourning his wife, to Cole's story of having fame and fortune stripped away, the games had a way of really making you care. When Anya sits down on the beach next to Marcus at the end of *Gears of War 3*, you're sad for them. Sure, they're probably gonna bone as soon as the credits roll, but that's not what you're focused on. In the moment, you're just happy that Marcus had a friend to lean on.

To this day, Dom's death remains one of the most memorable moments of any video game I've played in my life. Rest in peace, Dominic Santiago.

* * *

Learning that Epic Games had sold the *Gears of War* license to Microsoft in 2014 was nearly as depressing as seeing Dom go up in a ball of flames. I wasn't particularly worried about the games' quality declining since Microsoft smartly put Rod Ferguson in charge of the studio taking over development. No, I was concerned about something more personal. Namely, that the level of support we received at Epic wouldn't continue.[38] And two years later, when I was given the name of my contact at The Coalition, the studio developing *Gears of War 4*, those fears were realized.

The project nearly made me swear off writing guides forever.

Epic Games, more than any other developer I worked with, ensured our guides were complete. It's as simple as that. Too many companies acted less a partner in the guidebook's creation and more of an obstacle needing to be smashed through or avoided entirely. Every author had his or her share of horror stories, but it almost always came down to withholding content.

The only time Epic Games dissuaded us from including information concerned the Easter eggs in *Gears of War 3*, specifically the sequence for unlocking the giant golden chicken aboard the ship. Fine. Secrets of that sort didn't affect gameplay or have any connection to achievements, so it was a simple compromise.

The same can't be said for the Data Pads in *Halo: Reach*, which were among the best-hidden collectibles I'd encountered in any game I had covered. Bungie wanted no mention of them in our book, despite

---

[38] That being said, robots? Really? SMH.

ieir being an achievement linked to finding them all. The gamer in me
new this was bullshit. How could we sell a book that didn't cover one of
ie trickiest aspects of the game?

Fortunately, our contact at 343 Industries, the ever-helpful
orrinne Robinson, persuaded Bungie to meet me halfway. They
eluctantly allowed me to include a list of cryptic clues to the 19 Data
'ad locations.[39] It wasn't ideal, but it was the best we were allowed to
o. I can only hope that the "community effort" Bungie hoped to foster
isted longer than it took someone to upload a video to YouTube.

Then again, at least YouTube existed in 2010.

That certainly wasn't the case a decade earlier when the guide
o *Final Fantasy IX* was published, a book industry journalist Jason
ichreier calls "the worst guide ever made." Nearly every page of the
;uidebook employed blue note boxes directing players to Square's
iurgeoning online portal, PlayOnline.[40] Tips for playing the game,
inlocking side quests, and discovering secret items were stripped from

---

[39] Considering the very first Data Pad is attached to the back of an
invisible enemy (an Elite with Active Camouflage) that runs away from
'he player in the game's opening moments (and only on Legendary
lifficulty), I knew omitting them entirely would be an unforgiveable in the
eyes of many readers.

[40] Square Enix re-released *Final Fantasy IX* for the Nintendo Switch in
February 2019, as I happened to be writing this chapter. Sadly, the
PlayOnline website is still completely devoted to *Final Fantasy XI*. Short
of discovering an archived copy of the original website somewhere, none
of the content stripped from the printed strategy guide can be found
online. Some say the Internet never forgets. That may be true, except
when you're paying for it to remember.

the guide and replaced with passwords. In order to access the missing information, readers had to log into an account on PlayOnline. It was the equivalent of going out to see a movie in which every major plot point and action sequence was replaced with instructions to watch it on your phone.

Theaters would be lucky if popcorn was the only thing burning by the end of the film.

BradyGames was already wrapping up work on the guide for *Final Fantasy IX* by the time I got called on to help with the *Tenchu 2* book, but the ordeal was much-discussed for years to come. In short, everyone involved with the strategy guide knew this was going to bite them in the ass. But Square was in control and nobody at BradyGames– not the publisher, the editor, and especially not the author—could steer them away from PlayOnline. BradyGames suggested alternative ways of co-branding the portal. They fought to minimize the amount of information being withheld. They tried limiting it to entirely optional, inconsequential content. Square would have none of it. Strategy guide publishing is, ultimately, a parasitic industry. We existed at the pleasure of the host. And back in 2000, Square was the fattest, juiciest meal of all.

Book publishers live and die by the sales of a handful of titles each year. And few franchises, especially in 2000, could slug it out with *Final Fantasy*. There was no way BradyGames could risk losing out on future *Final Fantasy* guides by going against Square's wishes regarding the PlayOnline matter. All guides are contractually required to get the icensor's stamp of approval before the book goes to print. No PlayOnline, no book at all.[41] And definitely no contract for *Final Fantasy X* the following year.

Decisions like this, driven by suits in corner offices, were well beyond the writer's purview. The author of the *Final Fantasy IX* guide, Dan Birlew, could only sit back and hope they didn't cut too deep. But what was even more frustrating, and what had me so concerned about *Gears of War 4*, was when the hurdle was a single individual, a gatekeeper so comfortable presiding over his fiefdom, he'd forgotten that he was supposed to be there to help.

Most projects were perfectly workable even without developer assistance. Take the guide for *Super Mario Odyssey* for example. Joe Epstein and I received no support from Nintendo other than early access to the game. Finding all of the coins, Power Moons, and other collectibles was entirely up to us. Granted, Mario doesn't have an arsenal of weapons with ballistic data or enemies with specific damage and health values to consider.

For most games, the data is king. I wouldn't be surprised if many gamers bought our books solely for firing rates, attack damage, and hit-point data. To them, the skirmish-by-skirmish walkthrough, multiplayer maps, and achievement guides were merely bonuses. This was particularly true for shooters like *Gears of War*.

---

[41] In speaking to BradyGames staff afterward, they knew readers were going to hate it—and they did. Fortunately, Square caught a fair bit of backlash too and knew better than to ever again force BradyGames to cannibalize a strategy guide.

Chris Mielke, my primary contact at Epic Games, was always quick to provide this info shortly after our arrival on site. Unfortunately, I wasn't given access to his counterpart at The Coalition. Instead, we had to deal directly with licensing. And nobody in our line of work would ever trade developer access for someone in licensing. Kevin Bacon is fewer steps removed than most of those people.

Making matters worse, I knew the guy, and his reputation preceded him. He proved so difficult to deal with on *Diablo III: Reaper of Souls* that when I learned he was now handling licensing for The Coalition, and would be my contact for *Gears of War 4*, I considered turning down the project.

Three weeks later, I wish I had.

Despite it being my favorite franchise, writing the *Gears of War 4* strategy guide ultimately proved so frustrating that I considered walking off the project.

Instead, I gnashed my teeth as my love of game and career suffocated in the empty vacuum of my inbox. No question directed to this contact was ever deemed worthy of a response. No asset request from either me or my editors failed to be ignored. With the deadline looming, and not a single map, artwork, or spreadsheet of ballistics data provided, I finally took to emailing around the studio asking his coworkers if the guy still worked there. That finally got a response—he wasn't pleased—but even then it took until he left on paternity leave for us to receive the requested assets; an intern assembled everything we needed in a single afternoon.

For those players who were sad to see Epic relinquish the *Gears of War* license, believe me when I say that I felt your pain.[42] But while the *Gears of War 4* strategy guide proved frustrating, I take solace in knowing I only had to write it once. The same can't be said for the infernal difficulty that was the biggest, highest-profile guide of my career.

---

[42] Obviously, Epic is doing just fine without the *GoW* franchise. My last time at their studio was in early 2013, to work on the guide for *Gears of War: Judgment*. At that point, I was curious about a game called *Fortnite* that was announced back in 2011, but one we hadn't heard much about since. I asked a few Epic employees about it, hoping I'd get to do a guide for it later that year. They each chuckled and told me not to hold my breath, that *Fortnite* wasn't likely to ever see the light of day. Though the game didn't officially release until July 2017, I think we can all agree that it's getting its fair share of the spotlight. The video game industry as a whole took in $12 billion back in 2006, the year *Gears of War* released. *Fortnite* alone earned Epic Games nearly $3 billion in 2018.

To Hell and Back

The first time I ever sat in a pitch meeting was for 2010's *Halo: Reach,*
project my ego—and bank account—was more invested in than my heart
The Microsoft licensor contact in charge of the meeting spread several
collector's edition guidebooks across the table and asked if any of us
representing BradyGames had worked on the titles she chose. I raised
my hand and said, "I wrote three of the four." Chris Hausermann
acknowledged that he had managed several of her selections. Book
designer Keith Lowe claimed similar, and Waybright, still head of
BradyGames, leaned back and all but put his feet on the table. The
meeting seemed a mere formality after that.

The 2011 meeting at Blizzard for *Diablo III* was far less casual.

Not only did I really want to write the book, but BradyGames
absolutely had to win that contract. Other than shooters like *Call of Duty*
Modern Warfare 3 and *Gears of War 3*, there weren't many best sellers

n Brady's publishing schedule that year beyond *Arkham City.* Making
natters worse, archrival Prima Games already had *Skyrim* locked up.

I joined Mike Degler for breakfast at the Irvine DoubleTree,
own the road from Blizzard. Degler, a lifer on the business side of the
ompany, had recently been promoted to the publisher role at
radyGames. He asked me to come prepared with suggestions that
ould wow the *Diablo III* team, ideas that tapped into my so-called
xpertise as a *Diablo* fan.

It was rare enough for an author to be invited to attend such a
neeting, let alone be asked to present ideas. I was flattered, but
ervous. The truth is that it had been more than a decade since I had
layed *Diablo II*, and even then only in small doses thanks to the crush
f projects I juggled in the early aughts. My experience with the
ranchise was primarily tied to the original game that released all the
vay back in December 1996. Though I was careful to never oversell my
kill in a given game or genre, I wasn't always so quick to correct any
verestimates on the part of others. If the folks at BradyGames wanted
o think of me as enough of a *Diablo* expert in whom to entrust the
uide, I wasn't about to object.

Instead, I crammed—and prayed nobody quizzed me on my
Diablo bona fides.

Unlike my initial visit to Nintendo eleven years earlier, the reality
f being on-site at Blizzard certainly lived up to the mystique. The
sprawling, manicured campus, completely encircled in spiky metal
fencing with security outposts, was simultaneously inviting and

imposing. The twelve-foot-tall orc statue outside the headquarters building was even more impressive than expected, the compass of core values surrounding it less groan-inducing. Beneath an array of colorful banners flapping in the southern California breeze, I watched as some of the industry's top talent hustled about, lanyards and ID badges slapping against their garish tee shirts, and wondered if I belonged.

Cold feet. Impostor syndrome. Whatever you call it, for the first time in more than a decade, I was nervous. Even worse, I felt myself growing indifferent. I'd heard the nightmare stories about the difficulties writing a guide for a Blizzard title. The constant delays, the unending changes and tweaks, and the inevitable barrage of patches that would render any printed data obsolete. And then there were the fans, an army of loyalists so numerous the studio had long since abandoned E3 in favor of their own three-ring expo called BlizzCon. I'd written plenty of guides for big games before, but none for a title with a fan base as exacting, as ravenous.

Was I up to it?

As I completed a slow lap around the orc statue, a tour group ambled past, a picket of selfie sticks raised in tribute. I watched as they snapped the requisite photos that would guarantee the hashtag envy of their guild mates—quest complete—and I was reminded how lucky I was. I'd found a glitch in the industry. This "fake job," as Joe Epstein is fond of saying, was the biggest and best gaming exploit ever, better than the shuffle technique in *Tony Hawk's Pro Skater*, more potent than a two-piece Gnasher blast in *Gears of War*. I'd hacked my way into a career in gaming with no programming or artistic skill required, no years of servitude in the QA coal mines.

I looked at the plaque before me and smiled. *Yeah*, I thought while reading the eighth core value, *I'm ready to embrace my inner geek.*

In the meeting, Degler passed out a half-dozen faux wooden boxes, each handcrafted by the staff in Indianapolis to resemble an ancient tome, like something Deckard Cain himself may have had on his bookshelf. Inside were a series of volumes with custom *Diablo*-inspired slip-covers. Ribbon resembling the in-game banners identified the various components of the pitch: ideas for the book, marketing and pack-in suggestions, and most importantly, the financials.

It was a gorgeous presentation. And one we were confident Prima Games couldn't possibly match, given that they outsourced the bulk of their design work to various digital freelancers. If Prima or Piggyback were going to beat us, it wouldn't be with creativity.

As independent contractors, we strategy guide authors were seldom privy to sales figures or anything concerning the financial arrangements between the guidebook publisher and the game companies. Aside from royalty statements showing whether or not my books ever "earned out," the only clue to their success was the occasional appearance in the New York Time Bestseller List or the Amazon Top 25.[43]

---

[43] The nature of my contract required BradyGames to treat my per-book fees as an advance, with one dollar from each book sale going toward

I wasn't surprised to sense Degler stiffen uncomfortably and look my way as the softer topics gave way to a discussion of money. But like a twelve-year-old watching an R-rated movie with his parents, I wasn't going to avert my eyes right when the sexy bits were about to be unveiled.

Whether the upfront licensing fee was half or a full million dollars, I can't remember. The number that stuck out the most, the one I still shake my head over today, concerned the escalating royalty rate. For background, the author of your favorite novel likely topped out at a 10-15% royalty, maybe 20% for a best-selling hardcover.[44]

As far as strategy guides are concerned, those numbers represent the floor, at least for *Diablo III*—and entries in the *Grand Theft Auto* series, from what I've heard. Beyond a certain sales threshold— 250,000 copies sold, if memory serves—BradyGames offered to pay Blizzard a royalty of 50 freaking percent!

Considering wholesale discounts to retailers routinely reach 55%, this offer, when taking printing costs into account, left little to no

---

my pay, for tracking purposes only. For this reason, I was sent reams of royalty statements over the years, providing insight into how many books sold at least 10,000 copies. I'd estimate one in five of the guides I wrote failed to sell even 5,000 copies. As for the best-selling guides, I have no idea how many they sold. Once they hit the 10,000 mark and "earned out," the statements stopped coming, as I wasn't due a royalty.

[44] Conversely, indie authors fetch up to a 70% royalty on eBook sales. So, if you bought this book for your Kindle, Kobo, or other digital device, thank you for your support.

money for BradyGames. They may have even lost money on each book sold beyond a certain threshold.

I didn't have much time to pick my jaw up from the floor, as it was soon my turn to field questions from Jay Wilson and Christian Lichtner, *Diablo III's* lead designer and art director, respectively. Lichtner quickly expressed concern about the quality of screenshots in a lot of our guides. Namely, how dark and muddy they often looked. It was an issue I'd long expressed frustration over. I explained that it was often due to inconsistent video capture quality from gaming consoles and the at-times lower grade paper the book was printed on. As I worked to assure him that being able to capture high-res screenshots from the PC would result in higher quality, Degler jumped in to promise the book would be printed on higher quality paper.

Whether we had successfully allayed Lichtner's concerns was unclear, but Wilson appeared bored with the conversation and wanted to hear my ideas for the book.

It was time to show why I was there. And despite my earlier reservations, I couldn't wait.

The *Diablo* franchise is an angels-and-demons-themed action RPG that challenges players to fight their way through myriad dungeons in effort to grow strong enough to ultimately slay the titular character. The game has nigh-infinite replay value thanks to its ever-increasing difficulty and the hunt for rarer treasure and weaponry, systems built upon a foundation of apparent randomness.

In preparing for the meeting, I learned that *Diablo's* trademark dungeons, despite appearing to be completely random to the casual player, were actually comprised of several dozen tile pieces, hand-designed for each region of the game world and thrown into a hopper. The game then built the dungeon quasi-randomly on the fly as the level loaded, assembling the labyrinth based on a litany of rules concerning each of the tiles. It's like playing Scrabble, but instead of letters, the game engine empties the silk purse of staircases, corridors, and palace halls in a single turn, building words in a proprietary language only the developers know.

Because randomness is the bane of a strategy guide author's existence—second only to multiple endings—I knew I needed a way to account for the fact that everyone's dungeon-crawling experience would be unique. I proposed prefacing each dungeon in the guide with "An Explorer's Journal" in which, alongside a few select pieces of dungeon architecture (i.e., the tiles), I would provide tactical advice in the form of a diary entry, written in the style of the game's dialogue, by an anonymous adventurer. Telling the game's lead designer that you're going to ape one of their main characters is a risky play, but I sensed these guys wanted to see something different, something that honored the game while being helpful

To further build upon the idea, I suggested running the chosen tiles through a barrage of effects to transform them into sepia-toned— and blood-stained—pencil sketches. It was fan service, for sure. But if done well, it could provide helpful tactical advice too.

Degler and I surveyed a row of blank faces for what felt like eternity as Wilson, Lichtner, and the rest digested what I'd served up. Then, one by one, they began to nod. Some even smiled. And I exhaled.[45]

That afternoon, back at the airport, Degler agreed that the meeting went as well as it could have, but we both knew it wasn't a sure thing. Then, in a comment that I can say held true to the last of days, he said, "Either way, as long as I have any say in the matter, you'll always have work from us if you want it." It was a comforting thing to hear, but I couldn't ignore the trace of despair in his voice. The elephant in the room was growing a second head. If we were going to continue doing this in the future, we didn't merely need to secure the *Diablo III* license. We needed to slay it.

* * *

---

[45] We'd later learn that Blizzard takes on projects like strategy guides only if the heads of the team feel a true passion for what is being proposed. It's not driven by the licensing department as much as it is by the owners of the product. In this case, Wilson and company. Learning this not only makes it easier to understand why I had to be involved in the pitch meeting—and may even channel some credit in my direction—but also explains why there was no guide for *Overwatch*. It wasn't about the money. Of course, it would have shipped thousands of copies and made Activision-Blizzard and Prima Games plenty of cash, but the heads of the *Overwatch* team likely didn't feel passionate about it, thus it was dead.

At the end of a featureless, whitewashed hallway stood a locked wooden door, unremarkable in every way save for the novelty road sign adorning it. Comic relief? A cheeky promise? In May 2011, nearly ten years into *Diablo III*'s development, the sign spoke a temporary truth: THERE IS NO COW LEVEL.[46]

Behind the door, the air changed. I remember it cooler, darker, pulsing not only with the electric thrum of so much computing power, but with the nervous energy of those creating what would become one of the best-selling games of all time.[47] Cool blue monitor light shone from within blacked-out cubicles and offices, bathing the programmers and artists, engineers and producers in a protective aura. In the distance, lit from within by LED hellfire, stood a towering statue of Diablo himself, The Prime Evil. Devotion was compulsory.

A lengthy wall divided the sector, adorned with printouts of the dozen-plus armor sets for each of the five character classes, from the loinclothed Barbarian to the stoneclad Witch Doctor. A blackout screen

---

[46] There was a secret level, of course, but I was forbidden from mentioning it. In fact, the very first time I inquired about a "Black Mushroom" I had found, I was told to forget I ever saw it. Later, when I asked about the Staff of Herding, I was told to strike it from the book. It wasn't until the *Reaper of Souls* expansion in 2014 that we were finally permitted to cover the rainbows-and-ponies land that was Whimsyshire. Of course, Whimsyshire wasn't technically a "cow level," as in *Diablo II*, but it served the purpose, all the while having a laugh with fans who were afraid early gameplay videos were too cartoonish.

[47] As of this writing, according to Wikipedia, *Diablo III*, including the *Reaper of Souls* expansion, is the fifth best-selling game of all time not to come bundled with a game console. It has sold over 30,000,000 copies.

remained rolled above the concept art, lowered only during press tours. An identical screen hung on an adjacent wall, forever unfurled, concealing the development timeline, or so I was told. Could a Gantt chart stretch a decade in length?

A Blizzard game is said to release "when it's done." I arrived hoping they were close.

One who knew, but wasn't at liberty to say, was Matt Panepinto, the production assistant serving as my contact at Blizzard. A flip-flop-wearing cross between Conan and Gimli, Panepinto was not only a font of knowledge, but also solely responsible for maintaining my haphazard connection to Battle.net. Muscular, bald, and heavily bearded with a commemorative sword within arm's reach, he cut an imposing figure. I hated to bother him—was almost scared to—but had little choice. So, I did. Often.

Thanks to titles like *Fortnite*, *Destiny 2*, and Blizzard's own *Overwatch*, many players no longer bat an eye when learning that a game requires a constant Internet connection. But back during the run-up to *Diablo III*'s release, this was a major point of concern for fans. That a single-player game would be unplayable offline drew even more ire than the game's beleaguered Auction House. Nevertheless, I assumed I'd be spared any hindrances, given that I'd be writing the guide on-site at Blizzard's headquarters.

Forgive me, my ignorance is showing again.

Over the years, we strategy guide authors grew accustomed to working from multiple builds when a game was still in development. It was even fairly common for save data to be incompatible between updates. Having to start over once or twice was seldom more than an inconvenience.

With *Diablo III*, it was a near-daily occurrence. New builds were uploaded to the Battle.net servers seemingly around the clock, piling atop one another until, inevitably, I'd be disconnected mid-dungeon. I'd sigh, walk down the hall, and timidly knock on Panepinto's door. Best case scenario, he'd follow me back to my workstation, log into a secure network I had no access to, and install the new version. If I was lucky, my game save would persist across a few builds, allowing a few days of progress. Too often, however, the problem was Battle.net itself. And I was but one of many affected by an indefinite stoppage.

These technical difficulties were a mere annoyance during my initial getting-to-know-the-game trip in May. They were downright maddening during my weeks-long visits later that year. I begged for weekend access, praying for two days' time with a stable build, but was denied.

By fall, I'd seen Act I so many times, I could have cleared it blindfolded.

Making matters worse was the need to play through the game four times, once on each difficulty, in order to reach the level cap and have a chance, well, *in Hell*, of staying alive on Inferno difficulty.[48] Yes, a

---

[48] The initial release of *Diablo III* bears little resemblance to how the endgame functions now. Keep in mind that this was before Paragon Levels, Nephalem Rifts, and the Bounties of Adventure mode.

obust debug system made it possible to create a character at any level instantly and jump to a specific chapter within the game, but that's not how I rolled. I was a firm believer that a strategy guide could be useful only if the author replicated the end-user experience. Auto-generating a level 53 Monk might save me from backtracking through the game for the umpteenth time, but how would I know what crafting upgrades players likely had at their disposal? How many Legendary weapons might they have? How could I recommend the best ways to socket their gems and spend their gold if I was respawning with none?

Every day, it was two steps forward, one back, gradually documenting the game's myriad side quests—also random—and building the walkthrough in between crashes, network errors, and reinstalls. Beside me, blissfully offline, Rick Barba poked and prodded hundreds of enemy variants in a development tool sandbox as he compiled the book's massive bestiary. And each night, back at the DoubleTree, we'd toast one another's misery—my frustration and his boredom, to be specific—with a round of Basil Hayden on the rocks. And then another for good measure. After all, BradyGames was buying.

A rumored September release became a wished-for holiday surprise which, in turn, drifted to February, then again to May, a full year after my first spin with the Demon Hunter. By then, I'd spent nearly three months at Blizzard, split across a half-dozen trips. Every time we packed our bags, we thought it would be for good. That we'd head home, polish the text, and be paging through the finished book a month later.

But, in the eyes of Blizzard, it wasn't done.

Rick and I were ordered back time and again, our fingers crossed in hope that the game's evolution wouldn't require a full rewrite. Rick knew better than to finalize bestiary and item data before the very last minute. Thankfully, the additions to the campaign were relatively minor. Too bad the same couldn't be said for the skills system.

Like monster data, I expected the numbers to change right up to—and beyond—the game's release. What I didn't expect, however, was wholesale revamping of the skills system. At the end of each three-week stint on-site, I'd spend the final days hurriedly transcribing each hero's active and passive skills. More than a hundred pages of manuscript. And every time I returned, I'd discover, much to my horror, that the skill system had been overhauled. An early version contained an inventory-choking rune system (similar to the gems). A later version forced the player to choose a permanent upgrade, *à la* a skill tree. Then, finally, the team settled on the rune system that the game shipped with.

The gamer in me found *Diablo III's* evolution fascinating. The team's commitment to getting it right was inspiring. But a big part of me couldn't wait for the book to be done. Little did I know, I'd still be writing *Diablo III* guides two years later.

* * *

Diablo III was a record-smashing success, selling an estimated 3.5 million copies in twenty-four hours, no small feat for a PC exclusive. To this day, it remains the fastest-selling computer game of all time, having old 10 million copies in its first three months. And over 14 million nique players took up arms in defense of Tristram within a year of its elease. Our guidebook sold comparatively well, anchoring itself in the mazon Top 25 throughout the launch window.

But the work was far from over.

Plagued by launch day network errors, fan dissatisfaction with he endgame experience (or lack thereof), and the polarizing real-money uction House, Blizzard's staff had no time to celebrate. Patches came ast and often, addressing the core PC fan base's complaints while more ignificant tweaks were incorporated into the console release. Additional hanges were made, eventually culminating in a complete overhaul of he loot system, released in tandem with the *Reaper of Souls* expansion n 2014.

Aside from the core campaign, the *Diablo III* players know today ears little resemblance to the one covered by the 496-page hardcover guide I co-wrote in 2012.

To bridge that gap, BradyGames sent me Thom Denick, a true-ife *Diablo* expert to aid in leveling-up the initial guide for the 2013 console release. While I busied myself updating text and replacing the screenshots for the campaign, Thom reworked many of the peripheral hapters, particularly the equipment section, ensuring it would be useful for advanced players. Then, in January of 2014, we joined forces again for the *Reaper of Souls* expansion. We stripped every page down to its core and rewrote the guide to focus on the newly-added Crusader class, Act V, endgame content, and the celebrated Loot 2.0 system.

And yes, we finally even got to cover the so-called cow level, Whimsyshire.

After so many months writing—and rewriting—the original book, having to tear it all down and rework it was bittersweet. Writing the guide for *Diablo III* was a labor of love. It was also a grim reminder of the Sisyphean challenge of producing printed documentation for a modern game. No matter how many nights I spent away from home, no matter how many times I updated my text, the finished book could only ever reflect a snapshot in a game's life. And the more successful the game, the faster it would evolve beyond the scope of our book. Could we ever keep up?

The rear cover of our *Diablo III: Reaper of Souls* guide exclaims "So begins the end of all things ..." in reference to the expansion's introduction of Malthael, the Angel of Death. That was but one of many ends being referenced. For BradyGames, it was acknowledgment of the merger between Penguin and Random House, the parent companies set to oversee the inevitable shotgun wedding between ourselves and archrival Prima Games.

On a personal level, the symbolism went deeper. *Reaper of Souls* was the first strategy guide I wrote outside of an annual contract in a dozen years. And at the time, I was all but certain it'd be the last to ever bear my name.

We Had a Good Run

I had learned not to expect surprises during my annual contract negotiations. In fact, referring to them as negotiations is downright absurd. The details concerning my compensation solidified in 2009 and remained identical for years to come. In 2011, my attempt to unlock even a token twenty bucks extra per book had failed. Which was odd, I thought, when later that month, I received Tim Bogenn's contract by accident. Lo and behold, they were paying him exactly twenty-five dollars per title more than what they paid me.

I didn't mind. Honestly. Good for him, I thought, amusing myself with the notion of it being a contractual obligation, perhaps even a longstanding finder's fee: $N + \$25$, where N equaled whatever they paid me.

This isn't to say I didn't look forward to my November calls with Leigh Davis, the editor-in-chief. We typically spoke by phone only once or twice a year, and these annual wrap-up calls were my best opportunity for feedback. More importantly, I was always keen to learn which licenses they had secured for the upcoming year—and anxious to lobby for any of the AAA titles that interested me. During our 2012 call, that meant discussing *Bioshock Infinite* and *Gears of War: Judgment*.[49]

Whether we ever got around to talking about the titles I'd write that next year, I can't remember.

Leigh thanked me for all my hard work on *Diablo III* and for the six weeks I begrudgingly spent at Gearbox Studios working on *Borderlands II* with Joe Epstein.[50] What she said next wasn't completely unexpected, yet it was the first spoken acknowledgment of the coming end of strategy guides. She said they'd renew my contract under the same terms for 2013, "But this is the last year we can offer contracts. I'll keep you as busy as I can in 2014, but beyond that," she sighed. "I just hope we have a job."

As sad as it was to hear the concern expressed aloud, that the strategy guide business was indeed being squeezed out by the likes of

---

[49] I actually began working on *Bioshock Infinite* earlier that fall, driving from a friend's wedding in New Jersey to Boston, Hurricane Sandy lashing my rental car as I crossed Rhode Island. The risk to body and possession was all for naught, as the game was nowhere near the state in which I needed it to be in order to write the guide.

[50] Begrudgingly, because of the time away from the Pacific Northwest in the middle of summer. To Dallas, no less. One doesn't tolerate eight months of gray and drizzle so they can be sent to Texas in July. Working side-by-side with Joe was the only saving grace. Well, that and the fact that the game was fantastic! Having worked on each of the *Borderlands* guides, and knowing that *Borderlands 3* will be unveiled at PAX East sometime this weekend (I'm write this on March 14, 2019) fills me with melancholy, knowing I won't be a part of it.

ouTube and Twitch, I felt a selfish sense of relief. As far as I was concerned, the timing was perfect.

My wife and I were gearing up to take a mini-retirement in 2014. In short, we aimed to quit our jobs, sell everything we owned, and travel the world by bicycle for a few years.[51] No more writing travel guides to fictitious places. Instead, I was gonna go on a true adventure! IRL, as the kids say.

We'd been planning and saving for years. And more than I feared being hit by a car or assaulted in a foreign land, my biggest concern was timing. I'd somehow made the Starbucks bumper sticker slogan a reality. I did what I loved and loved what I did. Authoring strategy guides was too great of a gig to walk away from while the getting was good. And not necessarily because of the money, but because of the freedom this wonderful career afforded me.

I was in my mid-thirties, holding a resume bursting with more than a hundred published books. I'd spent the bulk of my career working from home, setting my own schedule and, most importantly, doing something I (usually) loved. We weren't willing to postpone our round-the-world adventure indefinitely—we wanted to leave sooner than later—but I was terrified of pulling the ripcord prematurely.

Leigh's confession that 2013 would likely be my final year under contract was the green light we needed.

---

[51] We chronicled the trip at the blog, TwoFarGone.com. More significantly, the journey ultimately inspired my novel, *Tailwinds Past Florence*, a road-tripping love story with a time travel twist. Available everywhere books are sold.

So, in between acquiring gear and curbside meetings with Craigslist bargain hunters, I hustled. I actively requested every project that would require working on-site, banking hundreds of thousands of Hilton Honors points in the process. From *Bioshock Infinite* in January to *Dead Rising 3* in October, with trips to Epic and Blizzard in between, I was always on the road. And then, after three quiet winter months, I flew down to Orange County one final time for the *Reaper of Souls* expansion and a quick fifteen grand before pedaling off into the sunset. It was March 2014.

But, as is wont to happen in this digital world, predictions of the guidebook industry's demise had been sort of, kind of, mildly exaggerated.

* * *

Two years and twenty-two countries later, I checked in from Bali.

The Penguin Random House merger had claimed the jobs of many talented people as redundancies were eliminated between the two strategy guide imprints. In short, the former rivals coalesced beneath the Prima Games brand, maintaining the editorial and design staffs from BradyGames and the sales and marketing teams from Prima.[52] Only a handful of my former colleagues remained, but one still standing was Tim Fitzpatrick, recently promoted to managing editor.

---

[52] After so many years spent poking fun at what I saw to be a general laziness in Prima's guides, it was really hard to get used to writing under

Tim and I caught up from far sides of the world in that awkward way it can be for work friends who seldom see or talk to one another. I eventually got around to inquiring about taking on some guidebook projects when we returned home. Not like what I used to do, I explained. Just two or three books a year to keep some money coming in while I worked on a novel.[53] No marathon projects, a supporting role would be fine. The smaller the game, the better.

Despite the combined author pool and fewer titles being published, Tim said he'd keep me busy. And a few weeks later, in the spring of 2016, he served up exactly the kind of project I was hoping for. Bethesda Softworks had unexpectedly agreed to a strategy guide for *DOOM* at the last minute. I was offered the multiplayer section. The catch? I had only ten days to write it.

Thank God for bots.[54]

---

their logo. It was even harder to see our own layouts and designs grow simpler, staler.

[53] Though I fully intended to write a travel memoir about our bicycle adventure, I got the idea for a novel while cycling through the Pyrenees. Then, after spending months studying storycraft and outlining the book, I got to work. *Tailwinds Past Florence* released in January 2019. A sample is included in the rear of this book.

[54] The *DOOM* multiplayer project was particularly beneficial as a first project back in the saddle, in that I had to adjust to playing games again. In my two years of travel, I spent little time playing games. Though I dabbled in *Hearthstone* for a while, the only games I played semi-regularly were *Fire Emblem* and *Animal Crossing: A New Leaf* on the Nintendo 3DS. I didn't take a handheld system with me on the bike tour, but my wife spotted a number of my guidebooks translated into Italian in

I received a similar request several weeks later. Could I spend a week at Nintendo, helping with the *Splatoon 2* multiplayer guide? Absolutely. This was perfect, I thought, thrilled that I was able to assist in such short, intensive bursts. No project creep, no hassle. Get in, get out, get back to work on my novel. I couldn't believe my luck.

Then came *Gears of War 4* and my rose of a gig had lost its bloom. For a while, all I could see were the weeds sprouting up, choking my joy.

For starters, the money just wasn't there anymore. At least not for shooters. That I earned only half what I had made for each of the prior *Gears of War* books made dealing with our absentee contact all the more frustrating. But it wasn't just about the money. The books no longer felt special. Stunning, title-specific designs in which no two pages were alike had given way to generic, almost sterile layouts. Costs were trimmed, yet the price tags for the books crept ever higher.

Most bewildering of all, page counts were now dictated by the sales team's desired retail price instead of editorial expertise. For larger titles, like the guide to *Super Mario Odyssey* I wrote in 2017 with Joe Epstein, this meant seeing smaller type, less art, and fewer screenshots to avoid producing too large a book. The days of 400-page door stoppers were over. Yet for other titles, like *Harvest Moon: Light of Hope* and *Darksiders 3*, both of which I wrote in 2018, this required gratuitous stretching. With no input from the author, the sales team decided each

---

a GameStop in Livorno, Italy and, taking it as a sign, insisted on buying me a 3DS for Christmas.

book would release as 352-page hardcover collector's editions—with forty-dollar price tags to match!

Despite including eighty pages of nostalgic fluff celebrating the twentieth anniversary of the *Harvest Moon* series, the finished book barely reached 256 pages. Yet, it still cost as much as the game! I warned my editor that *Darksiders 3* was too simple to possibly necessitate a 352-page book. But once again, rather than reduce the price and embrace an organic page count, the book's content was stretched tissue thin. The 304-page book was littered with full-page screenshots and a redundant map section in effort to justify a $39.99 sticker.

There may well have been reasons for this that I wasn't privy to. The rising cost of paper and shipping couldn't have helped. Neither did the sudden increase in tariffs on printed goods coming out of China.[55] But we were competing with free. How does one expect to compete with free by raising prices and lowering value? It wasn't just us authors scratching our heads. The BradyGames veterans in editorial, design, and production repeated these arguments to the sales team and upper management until they were blue in the face, to no avail. Again, the lack of gamers on the business side of the company proved detrimental—no wonder Prima Games entered the merger with $11 million worth of red ink on the books.

---

[55] Not a concern prior to the merger, when BradyGames used a local print shop right there in Indiana to do their printing.

And, with few exceptions—the *Super Mario Odyssey* and *Now You're Playing With Super Power* books, for example—many of the titles worked on or learned about following my return home were absolutely of lesser quality. Smaller teams of authors, often working with diminished morale, were allotted ever shrinking time lines to do their job. Whereas the BradyGames printers were local and accommodating, PRH brass insisted post-merger Prima Games bend to the will of a corporate production team in New York City. It became standard practice to grant the printing and manufacturing staff more time than the authors were given to actually write it. All the while, Prima Games continued to cannibalize book sales with free tips articles, videos, and mini-guides on their website.

One needn't consult a Magic 8 Ball to see that all signs pointed to the business closing. That we survived past 2017 was astonishing. Capcom had decided to cease supporting strategy guides; we'd seen Blizzard walk away from a dump truck full of money that a guide for *Overwatch* would have netted; and few of the developers we still worked with seemed to care at all. Shortly after our *Super Mario Odyssey* book went to print, late in the fall of 2017, Prima Games underwent another round of layoffs. A handful of full-time employees remained, of which only one or two even played video games.

Somehow, despite failing to land the license for a *Red Dead Redemption 2* guide, things appeared to have turned a corner by the end of 2018. Prior to even finishing *Darksiders 3*, I was already tapped to write the books for *Days Gone* and *Ghost of Tsushima*—and was first n line for *Shenmue 3* if Prima got the license. Other authors were

ooking forward to *Last of Us 2* and *Sekiro: Shadows Die Twice*, among

others. All of a sudden we were miraculously awash in incredible

orojects, racing into 2019 on the momentum of the *Super Smash Bros

Ultimate* guide.

Then, in November 2018, a bomb exploded in my inbox. Prima

Games was closing.

I needed to sit down. Scratch that, I needed to breathe.

The one job I'd known for nearly twenty years was gone, snuffed

out via email by someone I never heard of in a London office I never

dealt with. I was a freelancer, a mere independent contractor, but I bled

BradyGames orange. I felt robbed, hurt, and scared. Despite bracing for

this moment for years, knowing the nature of modern gaming and online

media would inevitably curb stomp us into oblivion, there was no

oreparing for how disappointed I felt when it finally happened.

The only surprise was that I was somehow surprised.

Mike Degler called two days later to commiserate, to thank me

for my hard work, and to wish me well. Like a good captain, Degler

fought long and hard to keep the ship afloat. And like a lot of us, he

understood what the industry was losing. And he shared in our

mourning.

Strategy guides weren't like magazines. They weren't

disposable, least of all for people of a certain age, those who grew up

with guides spread across their laps while they sat playing *Ocarina of

Time* or *Grand Theft Auto III*. Or, in my case, *Kid Icarus* on the NES. For many of us, these guides were fundamental pieces of video game culture. They were anchors to some of our best memories, teachers illuminating aspects of our favorite games that we'd never have known otherwise. While playing, we referenced their maps and their boss battle tactics and scanned for hidden items. Away from the console, we thumbed the artwork, read the developer interviews, and studied bestiary data. We kept them on the shelf for years to come, their spines reminding us not necessarily of the author's words, but of our mastery of the games.

I have no doubt that the march toward direct digital purchasing hastened the demise of strategy guides. If players needn't visit a store to buy a game—physical or online—they weren't going to make a special trip for the guidebook. Yet, as gaming continued to embrace digital media, these strategy guides remained the one thing that gave them heft, that allowed our hobby to still feel tangible. All the gameplay trailers and Twitch streams and Reddit threads in the world can't replace the magic of holding a book.

Or maybe I'm just naive.[56] They say information is the new currency. And when it comes to video game tips, there are no exchange rates or transaction fees. Digital information is as plentiful as the air we breathe—and every bit as free. So long as people are willing to share it.

---

[56] I offered to send a twenty-something cousin of mine a free copy of the limited edition version of our *Super Mario Odyssey* guide after seeing him comment on how much he enjoyed the game. He turned it down. "That's what YouTube's for," he said. Ouch.

Maybe there will be a resurgence one day. Even if only as a fad like oxygen bars. Or perhaps those raised on free gameplay tips will demand a premium alternative. Like bottled water, satellite television, and streaming music. After all, if there's one thing our modern society excels at, it's convincing people to pay for what was once free.

But probably not. And that's okay. The largest player in the market made it to 2019 with several longtime BradyGames employees seeing it through, and many of the longest-tenured authors penning the final books that went to print, twenty-five years after publishing their first guides.

It was a good run, indeed.

New Chapter Plus

I've never been shy about what I did for a living. Quite the opposite, actually, as I spent much of my career in a perpetual pinch-me-I-must-be-dreaming state. As such, I got used to answering questions about strategy guides. Tons of questions. So, in effort to get out in front of some of the emails or DMs I might receive after this book is published, I thought it'd be fun to catalog the most common questions I've heard in an achievements-themed FAQ section. One last chapter, for old time's sake.

That said, if you have a question that I don't cover here, be sure to reach out via my website www.dougwalsh.com and consider subscribing to my mailing list. All subscribers receive a free digital copy (oh, the irony) of my travel memoir, *One Lousy Pirate*, and they are privy to special offers and exclusive previews of upcoming content. No spam, promise.

Now, on to the DougFAQs!

You Never Forget Your First: *What was the first official strategy guide you wrote?*
Well, if you recall way back in Chapter 2, the very first official guide I worked on was *Tenchu 2: Birth of the Stealth Assassins* with Tim Bogenn. This game appeared on the original PlayStation.

No More Training Wheels: *What was your first solo strategy guide for BradyGames?*
I co-authored three titles with Tim Bogenn and was then given a chance to solo the book for *Mat Hoffman's Pro BMX* in 2001. My first solo effort on-site at a game company was *Mario Kart: Super Circuit* for the Game Boy Advance, also in 2001.

Out With a Bang: *What was the last strategy guide you ever wrote?*
Though I didn't know it at the time, my final strategy guide project ended up being *Darksiders 3*. I had written the guide to the original game nearly nine years prior. Writing the book for the initial game was a far more enjoyable experience, thanks to a more polished build and better developer support. My copies of *Darksiders 3* were so plagued with bugs and glitches, I couldn't even access the final boss until past my deadline. In hindsight, I would have preferred *Super Mario Odyssey* as my swan song.

Easy Money: *What was the fastest project you ever completed?*

I wrote the entire guide for *Kelly Slater's Pro Surfer*, from start to finish, in five days. The blitz earned me over a thousand dollars per day (pre-tax, of course). As a last-minute support author, I was enlisted to help on the *Super Mario Sunshine* project for three or four days. Most projects took much longer.

Embrace the Grind: *What was the longest project you ever worked on?*
My involvement with the original *Diablo III* guide lasted almost a full year, including five trips totaling nearly ninety days on-site at Blizzard Entertainment in California. The original guide that released in May 2012 ended up counting as three books for my 2011 contract and two books for my 2012 contract. Nothing else even came close.

Worst. Game. Ever.: *What was the worst game you had to write a guide for?*
Despite having released back in 2005, *Death by Degrees*, the Nina Williams (*Tekken*) spin-off still haunts my sleep. This espionage-themed brawler for the PlayStation 2 was so bad, I distinctly recall submitting the final chapter along with a note to my editor that read "I still have no idea how to play this game." Hilariously, one of the reviews for my guide reads: "I like the book, however I just need the game to work for me so I can use the moves that are in the book." You and me both, sir.

High Fidelity: *What are the top five games you wrote guides for?*

First of all, thank you, imaginary interviewer, for not asking me to pick only one. That's kind of you. It's entirely subjective, of course, but I'd say the best games I got to write guides for include *Super Mario Odyssey*, *Bioshock*, *Gears of War 3*, *Legend of Zelda: The Wind Waker*, and *Batman: Arkham Asylum*. Honorable mentions to *Halo: Reach* and *Borderlands 2*.

U Got Good: *What was the most difficult game you wrote for?*
This is a tie, but for different reasons. *Tactics Ogre: Let Us Cling Together* was an incredibly hard project because of the game's scale. Even with a co-author focusing on the main campaign, I sank over 300 hours into this project covering the side quests and unlockable characters. For pure difficulty of play, I'd have to say my most challenging task was achieving Rainbow-V ranks for every level in *Viewtiful Joe* and *Viewtiful Joe 2*. I loved those games something fierce, but they nearly broke me.

No Sales for You!: *What was the worst selling guide you ever wrote?*
Trick answer! My guide for *Gotcha Force* ultimately never went on sale, despite receiving a small print run and being given away for free. *Gotcha Force* was a squad-based brawler/shooter involving teams of capsule toys. I was really bummed when the guide failed to receive proper distribution, as it was a pretty fun game if you put the effort into learning its intricacies. I wrote dozens of squad recommendations fitting every play style I could imagine. Even tactics for an all-medic team!

I'm Too Old For This: *What was the most juvenile thing you encountered?*

Poo Snakes. Of all the crazy sentences I've had to write over the years, from recommending players chainsaw enemies in *Gears of War* to describing the vicious combos of *Mad World,* typing the words "Poo Snake" dozens of times while writing the guide for *Blue Dragon Plus* has to top the list of gratuitous absurdity. The game featured Blue Poo Snakes, Iron Poo Snakes, Golden Poo Snakes, and every color and metal in between.

You Loathsome Beast: *What memories cause you to grind your teeth the most?*

Our book for *Tales of Vesperia* was not good. Jennifer Sims and I did the best we could with little to no developer support, no maps, and no JP guide to crib from. A glance at the reviews today shows how much content we missed. But that's not why I hate it so. The two months I spent working round the clock on this impossible book prevented me from adequately training for the Leadville 100 mountain bike race. I'd managed to squeeze in only a single ride of more than four hours that entire summer thanks to *Tales of Vesperia*, which left me grossly unprepared for such an intense event. I ended up completing the hundred-mile race in just over twelve hours, missing the coveted belt buckle by three lousy minutes. I blame Namco Bandai.

Pleasant Surprise: *What game wound up being better than you expected?*

I wasn't happy to learn I'd be doing the guide for *Halo: Reach*. In fact, I was downright pissed off about it. I didn't like *Halo*, hated *Halo 2*, and had long since sworn off the series. But, I had a job to do and tried to get my head right. I played through *Halo: ODST* and *Halo 3* in preparation, really enjoying the former and finding the latter mildly better than meh. I never anticipated *Halo: Reach* would be as good as it was, or that it would ultimately be one of my favorite games of the Xbox 360 generation—and one of the books I'm most proud of.

Unhappily Ever After: *What game were you most disappointed in?*

I don't take any joy in saying this, as it was the final game for the studio that made it and the culmination of one of my favorite franchises, but I found *Bioshock Infinite* to be a huge disappointment. Particularly, the second-half gameplay and nonsensical "it's quantum" story explanations.[57] I got to revisit the trilogy—and all of the corresponding DLC—while compiling the guide for *The Bioshock Collection* in 2016 (and

---

[7] While on-site at Irrational Games, whenever my co-author Logan Sharp or I had a question pertaining to the plot, any of our various studio contacts would just smugly shrug their shoulders and say, "It's quantum." The studio acted as if the theory of quantum physics gave them permission to confuse the player and leave plot holes unfilled. While the ending between Booker and Elizabeth does a fair job wrapping things up in a way that becomes less confusing with each successive playthrough, I can't help wondering how many players lost interest along the way.

updating all of my original screenshots and text). My takeaways: the *Bioshock 2: Minerva's Den* DLC was the best *Bioshock*-related content of the entire lot. And *Bioshock Infinite* had incredible potential spoiled by the desire to appeal to the *Call of Duty* crowd. It wasn't a bad game by any means, but one I found quite disappointing after the brilliance of the earlier games.

Next Stop, Pulitzer: *Did you ever work on any non-strategy guide projects?*

Yes, I did! One of my favorite projects was writing the *Making of Guild Wars 2* which, unfortunately, was available only to those who purchased the collector's edition of the game. I spent two weeks at ArenaNet in 2011, conducting more than thirty hours of interviews, playing the game, and browsing through myriad pieces of artwork to ensure that I covered all aspects of the game development process.

Sweet Swag, Bro: *Did you get a lot of free games?*

Unfortunately, no. Some game publishers would send copies of the games we covered to the BradyGames offices, but the employees in the office would typically scoop those up. I did, at one point, have a massive stack of DVDs bearing beta code for dozens of games, but I threw them out. The only time I received a copy of a game was *Diablo III*. Blizzard was kind enough to send over a collector's edition box signed by the development team.

Stranger in a Strange Land: *What was the oddest studio visit you experienced?*

In 2009, I was fortunate enough to visit Platinum Games in Osaka, Japan. As an immense fan of *Okami* and *Viewtiful Joe*, I was thrilled to meet Hideki Kamiya, but the meetings were odd. For starters, my editor missed his connection in San Francisco, forcing me to attend the first day's meetings alone. Though I was there to discuss my work on the guide for the Wii's *Mad World*—a game I had already beaten—everyone at Platinum Games thought I was a journalist and grew quite concerned when it was clear I knew about bosses and other gameplay elements not yet made public. The other reason for the trip was to learn what I could about *Bayonetta.* Though I did receive a demo of the game, scheduling prohibited me from writing its guide. All wasn't lost, however, as I developed a deep love of visiting Japan and now make a point to return every other year. And whenever I'm in Osaka, I stare up at the Umeda Sky Building and wonder what brilliance Kamiya-san has in store for us next.

Missed Opportunities: *What games do you wish you got to write a guide for?*

Perfect segue. I'm really disappointed to not be writing the guide for *Ghost of Tsushima*, for two reasons. First, I enjoy learning about Japanese history, and everything about this game suggests it's going to be great. Secondly, I don't have a PS4. Writing the guide would have given me a chance to play it without having to buy a new console.

Looking back over the years, I was bummed not to get a chance to write a guide for *Shenmue 2* or the long-awaited *Shenmue 3*. It would have been great to have joined forces one more time with Joe Epstein on *Borderlands 3* and *Metroid Prime 4* as well. I guess I'll just have to enjoy them from the comfort of home like everybody else, which actually sounds kind of nice now that I mention it.

Free Sample

TAILWINDS PAST FLORENCE

The following is an excerpt from Doug Walsh's debut novel, a road-tripping love story with a time-travel twist. The novel was inspired by the two years he spent cycling the world, undertaking an adventure of his own, in the real world.

Chapter 1

Wednesday, February 11 — Seattle, Washington, USA

Edward Vaughan cursed the midday stillness as his wedding band tapped a jittery S.O.S. against the granite countertop.

He stood in the same spot every morning at five, mug in hand, scanning his news feed, checking the pre-market indicators. Even at that early hour, the apartment would buzz with Kara's presence. He'd kiss her forehead goodbye as she slept, anticipating another on her lips fifteen hours later to bookend his workday. She'd be in sweats and a tee, a cold, food-streaked plate beside her on the couch, wine glass within reach. His dinner would be waiting on the stove, the television chugging through a YouTube playlist on mute, a book unfurled on her lap.

That was their routine.

He'd never forget overhearing Kara on the phone, raving to a friend back east about the Space Needle views and luxury finishes when they moved in. Her excitement fueled him for months, but his tank needed a refill. Edward had hoped to surprise her tonight with a move to the junior penthouse. Now they couldn't even afford what they had.

Good thing the lease is up next month.

He adjusted his suit cuff and checked the time. She'd be home soon. He needed an explanation.

The words would come. Eventually. But he had to get moving. Fortune never favored anyone who stood around, going cross-eyed in an unlit kitchen.

Edward knocked the counter twice, gaveling himself into action.

He tugged the half-Windsor loose and undid the top button on his shirt. Custom or not, the damn collar had been strangling him since the drive home. He pulled off the jacket and kicked his shoes ahead down the hall. One took a bad bounce, scuffing the wall, ricocheting into Kara's studio.

The door was typically closed.

With no kids on the horizon or in-laws willing to travel *all that way*, the second bedroom had become a land of forgotten hobbies.

ust-covered mountain bikes leaned where a dresser may have stood, a
aint-splattered drop cloth took the place of a guest bed, an empty easel
lieu of a mirror.

As he rose from picking up the shoe, an unexpected absence
aught his eye. The map was gone. For months it had hung opposite the
oor, above a bookcase lined with old college texts and a copious
ollection of brushes and paint tubes. Now, in its stead, only thumbtack
oles in the same not-quite-white (Kara called it *Saffron Lace*) that
overed every wall in their Seattle apartment.

She brought the map home last fall, a laminated Rand-McNally
epicting every country on earth in shaded relief. Accompanying it was a
roposal to bicycle around the world. She wanted him to take a
abbatical—a laughable notion in the world of venture capital—and
pend a year or three traveling.

Issues of *Adventure Cyclist* appeared in the bathroom soon
fter, borrowed travel guides rotated across her nightstand, and
eemingly every conversation held an air of wanderlust, with Kara pining
or small towns and country roads, campfire beers at sunset. *Just the
wo of us,* she'd say in a coquettish whisper. *While we're still young.*
dward could only guess what spurred her restlessness and expected it
o vanish as abruptly as it emerged.

The map hadn't gone far. A quick search found it crunched into
football of discarded fantasy, punted behind a pile of bags and boxes.
3y the looks of things, she'd cleaned out the closet.

He unfurled the map, exposing a runaway squiggle of black ink. His eyes locked on the map's northwest corner, where a star marked the departure point. Home. From there, the line dipped and danced across the northern United States and Canada before dashing south from London to Spain. Onward it went, around the Mediterranean to Greece, Turkey, and beyond. Edward followed the trail, past a who's who of countries he knew nothing about, to China and Vietnam and a hand-drawn smiley face clear on the other edge of the poster, in Bali.

She'd given up on it. No. *She gave up on me.*

A car alarm echoed between the high-rises, drawing his attention. He carried the map to the living room window, trying to recall the last time she'd mentioned the trip. Several weeks, at least. Probably not since New Year's.

In no mood to deal with construction, he had parked the Audi on the avenue, lucking into a spot where he'd be able see it. The car looked fine from his seventh-floor perch, the alarm wasn't his, but he could have done without his cardboard box reflecting in the storefront window across the street. Security had weaved the flaps shut, and only the top of a small bamboo plant jutted from a torn corner. But he knew the contents intimately. Framed photos of Kara, his MBA diploma, a couple of airport business books, and a half-empty bottle of Johnny Walker Blue kept on hand for toasting new deals.

He wasn't so naive as to think he'd spend his whole career with one firm. After all, he was only twenty-nine. But he never thought the end would come like this. So soon. Over something so avoidable. He sat in his car for hours that afternoon, forehead on the steering wheel, wishing for a do-over, a chance to rewind time. Most of all, he yearned for an escape from having to tell his wife.

As the day's events played in his mind, Kara approached on the sidewalk below. She did a double-take, as if his early arrival home was so unfathomable she refused to recognize their own car.

Even in Seattle there's not that many RS 5s.

Edward watched her stare at the telltale box, saw the slump in her posture, the reach for her phone. He backed away as she looked upward, forgetting the tinted glass was all but impossible to see through from outside, especially with the lights off. Down the hall, his phone vibrated inside his jacket pocket, the silk doing little to cushion it against the hardwood floor.

Anxiety slipped the map from his grasp, spiriting it beneath the couch where all but Oceania fell claim to the dust-bunnies and darkness. The smiley face stared at him, his dismissal of her dream visible in the scars of its creased face.

She didn't deserve that.

Edward snatched the map from the floor as the phone ceased vibrating behind him. *She'll be home any minute.* His breathing quickened, jolted by the surge of an idea, a way out.

Rolling the map as he went, he ran to the kitchen and yanked open the refrigerator. Shifting aside milk, jelly, and a palette of condiments, he unbarricaded a bottle of champagne from the back corner, silently thanking his father for instilling in him the value of being prepared for an unplanned celebration.

He plucked champagne flutes from a cabinet and hurried to the door where he arranged them just so atop a cedar console. He studied the scene from all angles, even stooping low to imagine the effect from Kara's height as she entered. Above the table hung a painting of an orca leaping through a field of stars—a Wyland original. His first bonus check. Edward adjusted the gallery lighting so it twinkled against the crystal stemware.

Am I really doing this?

What choice did he have? Tell her they'd have to move, that he couldn't afford to keep them in Seattle anymore, that he got himself blacklisted throughout the city's financial community? There was no reason to put her through that when she spent months trying to sell him on the perfect alternative.

The elevator dinged, launching his stomach into a backflip.

His grip on the bottle and map tightened as the key slid into the lock.

How will I pay for it?

The deadbolt turned.

I'll figure it out.

Edward shuffled out of Kara's view as the door opened inward. He counted down from three, giddy with the excitement of his surprise gift. "Butterflies, cover your eyes!"

* * *

Kara clutched her chest as her breathing returned to normal. It was one thing not to know why he wasn't at work, it was another for him to be hiding behind the door. *What the hell, Edward.* She bent to pick up her dropped keys. "You're home." It came out more statement than question.

"Long story. Why didn't you cover your eyes?"

She raised her hands in answer. They held a gym bag, purse, keys, and an envelope she'd somehow forgotten about in the commotion. "You didn't give me any time," she said. Then, noticing the map—*her* map—and the champagne, asked, "What's all this?"

"This," he said, grinning like a schoolboy about to receive his first kiss, "is a change of plans."

Her mouth fell open as she processed what she was hearing. Kara spent months asking him to take time off, hoping he'd see how important the trip was to her, practically begging. She tore the map down after the holidays, after diplomatic overtures had failed. She'd been holding a bomb ever since, delaying the inevitable. Now, with her self-imposed deadline having come and gone, he wanted to do it.

Today? You've got to be kidding me, she thought, clutching the envelope, dumbstruck.

"I thought you'd be excited." His smile drooped.

"I ... I am," she stammered. "I think. You have to admit, it's a lot to swallow."

"You still want to go, right?"

Did she? It'd be an incredible adventure, a badge she'd wear the rest of her life. But, to Kara, cycling around the world was a means to an end. Her gaze drifted to the map, the promise held within its Sharpie itinerary. The promise of change, of resurrecting the man she married, her best friend and lover. For three years, it'd be just the two of them, reforging their bond against the anvil of the open road. And if her plan didn't succeed, if he returned to his workaholic ways when it was over, she'd at least know she tried.

Kara felt a warmth spread through her, sensed her lips curling on a wave of hope.

"That the mail?" Edward nodded at the envelope, a legal-sized manila job with a string clasp. He turned around to pry loose the cork, his enthusiasm returning.

"Yeah, it's nothing." She seized the opportunity to place it face down on the floor and covered it with her gym bag. She unzipped her softshell jacket and draped it over the top for good measure. The cork exploded from the bottle like a starter's pistol, sending a stampede of questions racing through her mind. She didn't know where to begin. His reversal was as dizzying as it was unlikely.

"I saw the box on the passenger seat." She decided to probe. "What's going on?"

"I'm done. I'm not going back."

"You got your sabbatical? What about the promotion?"

"It's not important," he said, handing her a glass, avoiding eye contact.

The job meant everything to him, and she could tell there was something he wasn't telling her, but wasn't this what she wanted? Absolutely. She brought the glass even with her chin. The bubbles erupted like fireworks, tickling her lips and nose while she thought it over.

Can we afford it?

Probably. Even if it was unpaid leave, they had to have enough saved up.

I'll need to quit my job.

She bounced from contract to contract every year, a glorified, monogamous freelancer. She could leave anytime.

Do I still love him?

She looked up at Edward, pondering the secrets behind his creased brow, recalling the passion they'd shared, convincing herself it could be that way again. Yes. She loved him. Ever since college.

Kara began to nod as she tilted the glass to her lips.

"Not yet. We have to toast."

* * *

Kara Vaughan," he said, taking her hand as he dropped to a knee. "Will you bicycle around the world with me?" She looked past him.

Embarrassed, cold feet, nervous? He didn't know. *Say yes. Say yes, dammit.*

"Are you sure it's what you want?"

He rose and stepped toward her, barely restraining his sigh. "I wouldn't be here if it wasn't," he said. "We'll leave next month, take advantage of the low snowfall, and spend the rent deposit on new bikes."

She bit her lower lip and stared at the floor.

"Wasn't this your dream?"

She nodded. "It was."

"So, let's do it."

"Are you sure we can afford it?"

"It'll work out," he said, knowing she relied on him to mind their finances. In truth, they spent as much as he earned. The rent, his car, the furniture. He had no idea how much he owed, only what his credit limits were. He figured there was enough for a year or two on the road if they were frugal.

He was tired of waiting. He cupped his hand under her chin and raised it, locking eyes with hers. "Say yes."

Her hesitation faded into a fit of nervous laughter. "Yes," she shouted, clinking her glass with his. "One-hundred percent, yes!"

Edward downed his champagne in a heavy gulp and wrapped his arms around his wife, squeezing her tight, knowing he'd dodged a bullet.

And as Kara squeezed him back, spasming with joy against his chest, a blinding flash of light flooded the apartment. Bathing him from all sides, it washed over him like a wave, immersing him in an otherworldly glow. It was fleeting, silent, and when he realized that Kara hadn't sensed it, he began to doubt its occurrence. But what he couldn't deny was the brilliance of the shade. He'd only seen it once before, in Kara's paintings. *Cerulean Blue*, she called it. *Latin for the heavens.*

Stay in Touch

Got a question or comment? You can reach me via www.dougwalsh.com. While you're there, consider signing up for my newsletter. Subscribers receive special offers, behind-the-scenes content, and news on upcoming releases. All subscribers also receive a free eBook.

Reviews are critical to an author's success and improvement. Please consider leaving an honest review at Goodreads or your preferred retailer.

Acknowledgments

Have you ever watched the credits scroll at the end of a AAA game? The names just keep coming with no end in sight. Hundreds, if not thousands, of people who had a hand in creating that piece of software. Someone's job was to ensure everyone wasl accounted for, the names spelled correctly, their just dues duly given.

I have no such person under my employ to ensure I don't screw this up.

Instead, I have my memory and a bookshelf lined with over a hundred strategy guides that I was a part of. If I'm being honest, every person who worked on either the guidebook or the game it covers deserves my thanks. Many of the people I owe my deepest gratitude to were mentioned by name in this book. Editors, authors, managers, developers, producers, and (most) licensing contacts all contributed to the longevity of my absurdly wonderful career.

In no particular order, I want to extend a warm, heartfelt show of gratitude to everyone at BradyGames. To Leigh Davis, Mike Degler, Tim Fitzpatrick, Christopher Hausermann, Christian Sumner, Tim Cox, Jennifer Sims, Ken Schmidt, David Bartley, Carol Stamile, Will Cruz, Brent Gann, Stacey Beheler, Keith Lowe, Dan Caparo, Brian Shotton, Tracy Wehmeyer, Doug Wilkins, Areva, David Waybright, Robin Lasek,

Janet Eshenour, and everyone on the business side who I never had the pleasure of working with directly: Thank you, each and every one of you!

As Leigh once said, I didn't always play well with others. Still, there's no substitute for a kickass co-author. Though we didn't work together much at all, I may not have ever made this wonderful journey without Tim Bogenn. Thank you, sir! To Philip Marcus, Rick Barba, Dan Birlew, Michael Owen, Jim Morey, Thom Dennick, Logan Sharp, and Kenny Sims, it was an honor sharing a byline with you. To my friend and frequent collaborator, Joe Epstein, you were a constant reminder to step my game up—let the record show that nobody did this work better than you. Fact!

Special thanks to my tremendous critique group who helped shape and improve this text. I'm fortunate to have the following rock stars in my corner: David Anderson, Chenelle Bremont, Natalie French, Sandra Rosner, and Jeff Weaver. And also, again, Tim Fitzpatrick for editing the manuscript and contributing several anecdotes.

Lastly, as with most everything I do, it wouldn't have been possible without the support and encouragement of my wife, Kristin. You're the best.

CPSIA information can be obtained
at www.ICGtesting.com
Printed in the USA
FSHW020819010519
57717FS

9 781732 746763